THE LAW OF THE SEA

THE LAW OF THE SEA

VOLUME – I

Edited with an Introduction by

U.N. GUPTA

ATLANTIC
PUBLISHERS & DISTRIBUTORS

Published by

ATLANTIC
PUBLISHERS & DISTRIBUTORS
B-2, Vishal Enclave, Opp. Rajouri Garden,
New Delhi-110027
Phones : 25413460, 25429987, 25466842

Sales Office
7/22, Ansari Road, Darya Ganj,
New Delhi-110002
Phones : 23273880, 23275880, 23280451
Fax : 91-11-23285873
web : www.atlanticbooks.com
e-mail : info@atlanticbooks.com

ISBN 81-269-0408-9 (Vol. 1)
ISBN 81-269-0432-1 (Vol. 2)
ISBN 81-269-0433-X (Set)

Printed in India
at Nice Printing Press, Delhi

CONTENTS

VOLUME I

VOLUME II

ANNEXURES

AGREEMENT

APPENDICES

INTRODUCTION

U.N. GUPTA*

01. Oceans have been intimately related to the civilizational progress of mankind.[1] The oceans are vast, beyond human imagination, and cover over 140 million square miles of the surface of the earth. The turbulent sea covering more than two-third surface of earth is no longer formidable awe-generating proposition for man. Every portion of ocean mass on the earth has been mapped and identified in the interest of man by navigation surveyors, ocean-cartography, penetrating remote sensors and satellite mapping technology. Man may not have been able to control the physical ferocity of the sea, but the prospects of the use of oceanic wealth and the utilization of the marine and oceans as also easier pathway for interaction with States scattered all-around the world, are making their impacts on developments in laws regulating human conduct on the surface, underwater as well as on the ocean floors. The law of Sea which regulates the navigation and use of the sea for the Nations has been undergoing tremendous changes by peaceful and consensus procedures, particularly since the end of Second World War. These changes do not relate only to the use of sea for warfare but also for the future disposition and utilization of the intrinsic wealth contained in them. All the States having a coastline are now directly interconnected through the sea routes and lay claim to the wealth of the sea adjacent to their coastline. Underdeveloped and landlocked States look forward to receiving some share of the exploits of deep-sea minerals. These developments have forged a new global feeling and

* Former Professor, Head of Law Department; and former Vice-Chancellor, University of Allahabad, Allahabad, India.

understanding of human relationships as a sort of family of man, particularly in the second half of twentieth century. Somehow, all States of the world have been united in laying down a consensus-based regime for the sea and have actually accomplished their purpose. With its longstanding background history a complete regime regulating all aspects of uses of the sea and oceans has become functional since 1990s.

Background for Documentation of Customary Law of Sea

02. Documentation or progressive codification process of customary international law can be traced to the limitations on irresponsible State sovereignty with respect to wars on sea, which practically started with the Pact of Paris of 1865 after the Crimean War (1852-55). The foundation for the customary law of sea was provided by Grotius who in his writings as a diplomat, had given the status of *res communis* and *res extra commercium* to the seas, meaning thereby that the seas being inexhaustible like air, were common and equal property of mankind and which by their very nature could not be appropriated by any sovereign as part of his kingdom. Earlier to Grotius, in the fifteenth, sixteenth and early seventeenth centuries Spain and Portugal had divided[2] the Indian, Atlantic and Pacific Oceans between them, and England had also claimed sovereignty over North Sea and Narrow Seas to the exclusion of other States. Following Grotius, Holland in the seventeenth century with the support of France, Britain and other maritime States engaged in exploration and occupation of New World, had eventually developed a different customary law of sea. The principles of freedom of navigation and freedom of fishing were equally available to all States of the world under this customary law. Subsequently, in nineteenth century, the freedom of laying submarine cables and pipelines were added; and, later in the twentieth century freedom of air, that is to fly airplanes, was added. The concept of territorial waters, sovereignty over gulfs and bays, was of common interest and its evolution was based on canon-shot range capability of States, in the interests of protection of coastal areas during peace as well as in wars. Of course, international interests in artificial Suez and Panama

Canals were based in the right of third States in the documented bilateral treaties of dispositive nature.

03. The warfare on sea became notably inhuman during First World War, particularly because of the indiscriminate use of submarines to sink enemy ships, the right to visit and search of ships exercised by belligerents to prevent flow of contraband goods to the enemy, and the enforcement of long-distance blockaders. These had substantially harmed, restricted and censored the freedom of navigation on high seas that was to be equally available to neutral states in war legally limited between two or more States. Similar, was the extensive use of laying sea-mines to prevent navigation to the enemy coasts and ports, and the subsequent emplacement of sensing instruments on seabed for detecting movement of ships for war purposes. The lapses of the customary rules of the navigation on high seas were accounted for and were embodied in the law of sea in the manner in which it developed subsequently.

04. Then, there is the use of oceans and sea for purposes declared to be illegal by the community of nations in peacetime. States have faced the situation of carrying of prohibited narcotics, evading of custom duties and tariffs, smuggling of prohibited goods into a country, like gold, wine, watches or arms into their territory by smugglers. The question has been whether States can intercept such activities while the smugglers are on high seas beyond the territorial sea. The answer has gradually developed in affirmative and is now regulated by one or more conventions on the law of sea. The piracy *jure gentium* has been ages old crime problem and its ban is documented from time to time that give wide jurisdiction to States. Further, there was the generally practiced institution of slavery that was recognized as legal within States. The trade in Negro slaves was a highly profitable international business for several centuries. The prosperity, industrial or agricultural, of Europe and America during the days of manual labour was widely based on such cheap labour. The USA had its Civil War (1861-64) based on this internal conflict leading to abolition of internal slavery. In slow steps the other States also banned the institution of slavery internally. Alongside, this was followed by prohibition of use of

sea navigation in furtherance of slave trade. Yet another rampant evil form of slave trading, the white slavery, involving export of white women to Americas, Middle East and to African States for marriage or housekeeping, by use of Sea navigation is now banned by the Conventions though not completely eradicated.

05. *Law of Sea after First World War*: Every major war in Europe has had its impact on the freedom of navigation in high seas beyond the territorial waters of the States. How far a belligerent ship could go near the coastal areas while chasing an enemy ship without violating territorial waters of a neutral State was a often raised question, or the exercise of the right of blockade by the belligerents restricted or made hazardous merchant shipping of the neutral States that led to protests and actions on the part of neutral States. Within the territorial sea in peacetime the coastal State exercised criminal jurisdiction for the crimes committed on the board of foreign ships also. In the area of warfare on sea rules, the devastating effect of the use of submarines had been felt on the freedom of navigation enjoyed by neutral States and on the rules regarding sinking of civilian ships only after and when the people on board were taken out or saved. Accordingly, the (unenforced) Treaty of Washington of 1922 had prohibited the use of submarines in destroying commercial and merchant ships. The London Naval Treaty of 1930 and the London Submarine Protocol, 1936, signed between major world powers of the time, *viz.*, United Kingdom, USA, France, Italy and Japan, extended the rules relating to sinking of merchant ships by warships on sea surface to submarines warfare also. These were subsequently proclaimed to be 'declaratory of international law' by a general treaty, the Nylon Agreement of 1937. Some States were reaching out of their territorial waters, called contiguous zones, for the enforcement of rules relating to protection of fisheries, prevention of smuggling of prohibited goods, etc. Both of these infringements of freedom of navigation or of fishing were matters of a relative nature.

05A. The exercise of jurisdiction on high seas for crimes committed on ships or otherwise also became a matter of controversy and so it attracted attention. The collision between ships has necessitated determination of international liability for negligence in ship navigation. The famous *Lotus Case,* decided by the Permanent Court of International Justice had highlighted the international dimensions of the problem. The subsequent conventions or treaties on the Law of Sea of 1958 and 1982 have resolved the contentious part of the problem.

06. *Law of Sea after Second World War:* As the Second World War ended in 1945 and the Cold War (1950-1992) developed in international politics, the Law of Sea had become a focal point of considerable interest. The reasons were mainly strategic from the point of view of both the great powers' rivalry and the commercial utility of oceans. The technological advancements had made both aspects formidable. Strategically and commercially, instead of being an obstruction, the high seas had become direct link for approaching the territories of friendly States alike. The Seventh Fleet of the USA has its base in Indian Ocean and South East Asia. Iraq and Afghanistan, both landlocked States in the Middle East, have been devastated in the past UN actions of 1991 and 2001 by the naval aircrafts taking off from aircraft carrier ships, thousands of miles away from the USA. In March 2003, during the unilateral armed action taken by the USA and UK alliance against Iraq, the missiles fired from the US fleet in the Persian Gulf, the Red Sea and the Mediterranean Sea effectively devastated military bases and civilian areas of Iraq. The big aircraft carriers, battleships, and submarines armed with ballistic missiles now expose States with a coastline to hostile designs of powerful States though these may be situated on the other side of the globe. The point is relevant since under the international law of the sea, the freedom of navigation is available equally to warships and to merchant shipping both in times of peace and war. The war games are based on the opportunity to demoralize the enemy and sea warfare is a zone for unnerving the enemy by blocking the supply of war materials, necessities of life and navigation to and from the enemy territory. Attack, sink or seize enemy ship or any ship with enemy destination is authorized law of war. Sinking of ships, naval or merchant, by aerial bombardment, sea-mines or by submarines has become a dangerous part of maritime warfare because it more than often leads to destruction

of civilians of the enemy or nations of neutral States. The 1949 Geneva Convention number II on the 'Amelioration of the Conditions of Wounded, Sick and Shipwrecked Members of Armed Forces at Sea'[3] covers sick, wounded and shipwrecked[4] naval forces, mobile medical units, hospital ships[5], medical transport ships,[6] doctors and nurses or search[7] units engaged in Red-Cross[8] nature of activities.[9] Reprisals[10] against the wounded, sick, and shipwrecked persons, the personnel, the vessels or the equipment protected by the Convention are prohibited. The provisions of IInd Geneva Convention, 1949, are mandatory and their violation is a war crime punishable in a variety of ways. Further, the curtailment of the use of high seas for war purposes to a limited degree has been agreed upon by the major powers through a Sea-Bed Treaty, 1971. The treaty[11] prohibits emplacement of nuclear and other weapons of mass destruction on seabed and ocean-floor and in the subsoil thereof. It essentially operates for the protection of normal shipping against the hazards of the weapons placed on the seabed that may get activated when a ship passes over them. In 1988, the U.N. General Assembly adopted 'Convention for the Suppression of Unlawful Acts against the Safety of Maritime Navigation'. The purpose of the convention is to prosecute and punish the perpetrators of crimes on ships who jeopardise the life, liberty and security of persons. Another important but premature or stillborn development on curtailment of freedom of high seas for war purposes, in favour of the nations of the region, has been in the proposals for the development of Indian Ocean as a Zone of Peace. The General Assembly had adopted resolutions that declared the desirability of making Indian Ocean a Zone of Peace.[12] However, since the Cold War has ended and there is no encirclement of Soviet Russia[13] by Western Powers, this move though not shelved, has made little progress.

07. *The Commercial Utility of Oceans*: The other important reasons for vigorous innovative attention on the Law of Sea after the Second World War were: (i) the long range sophisticated technology for fishing in oceans as far as 1000 miles away from dry land in order to meet the shortage of animal food for human consumption that was keenly felt in Europe after the Second

World War, and (ii) the technological advancement in underwater extraction of minerals and the drilling out of the oils from the sea bed. Both of these developments were universal and were triggered by two unilateral proclamations[14] simultaneously made by the USA in September 1945, giving turbulence to the over three hundred years old customary international law of the sea.

07A. The first of the US proclamations developed into the 'Doctrine of Continental Shelf'. Under this doctrine the sea margin upto the depth of 200 metres beyond territorial sea was declared to be within exclusive jurisdiction of the USA for extracting embedded minerals, tin or petrol, from the seabed but without curtailing the common right of States to the established freedoms of the high seas on the surface of sea. The geomorphology of continental shelf is that it is a gently sloping platform adjacent to the continental land mass and qualifies as an extension of land structure submerged in the sea. Beyond continental shelf come 'continental slope', then 'continental rise' and thereafter the 'deep sea'. Instead of contesting this unilateral or arbitrary assumption of such a title over continental shelf by the USA, all other coastal States adopted the process of making similar proclamations in order to ensure similar advantages for themselves and to prevent technologically advanced foreign States from exploiting minerals from their adjoining areas. India also claimed sovereign rights over the seabed and subsoil of the continental shelf adjacent to Indian territorial waters.[15] However, the dissatisfaction against the 200 metres depth principle for continental shelf arose from South and Central American States which have a steep inclination between their land mass and the sea, thereby leading to a thin continental shelf. Instead of 'depth criterion' these States projected a doctrine of Contiguous Zone extending to 200 miles beyond their territorial sea for the interests involved. It may be mentioned that the doctrine of continental shelf was not an arbitrary innovation but was based on scientific reasoning that had been taken into account and was accepted in documenting and codifying of the principle in international law subsequently.[16] The continental shelf in geological terms was explained to be a 'natural prolongation of the land territory of the mainland into the sea to the point it reaches the ocean floor', which lies at the depth of about 3000 metres. As such it was commonly asserted that the coastal State had a natural and legitimate right over the minerals and other natural resources found over or embedded in that natural prolongation. There was no objection and this argument was accepted and advanced by all coastal States while making similar claims for their 'national' continental shelf.

07B. The second proclamation simultaneously made in September 1945 by the President of USA laid down a national policy[17] with respect to establishment of conservation zones for the control of fisheries in areas of the high seas contiguous to the coasts of United States, by means of American legislative or treaty arrangements, as the exploration of the fisheries might warrant. This innovation in the three hundred years old law of sea was justified by the USA on the ground of the "inadequacy of present arrangements for the protection and perpetuation of fisheries resources". It was also asserted that fisheries faced depletion due to new methods and techniques adopted for intensified fishing over much wide sea areas. There was no denying of the fact that the new techniques and capabilities of fishing were seriously and adversely affecting the repletion or compensation of fish wealth of the sea by natural breeding processes. These measures for conservation of fisheries were to operate in the congruous zone applicable both on US nationals and foreign fishermen. However, as in the case of continental shelf care was taken by the proclamation to treat conservation areas as part of the high seas as before, that is, this was not to adversely affect the traditional right of free and uninterrupted navigation and other freedoms in the defined conservation zones of the high seas enjoyed by all other States of the world.

08. Although this proclamation adversely affected the right of fishing by fishermen of other States in areas of high seas which fell under the proclamation, yet it was not resisted but it led them, about 45 States with coastline, to make their own conservation contiguous zones for the fisheries which controlled or precluded other States from freely fishing there. The controversies arose only where the angular projection or

proximity of two or more States led them to claim overlapping areas of the same sea.[18] This led the UN General Assembly to convene a technical and legal conference to devise principles for harmonizing conflicting contiguous fishing zones. The International Technical Conference on Conservation of the Living Resources of the Sea held at Rome in April-May 1956 submitted a Report accordingly. This Report through International Law Commission became one of the bases for the 1958 Geneva Conference on the Law of Sea.

08A. The situation of the customary international law of sea in 1951-55 was a chaotic mix due to uncertainties created by the conflicting and overlapping unilateral claims made by States of continental shelf areas, contiguous zones for conservation of fisheries and varying claims[19] of territorial waters made by some States. These developments had been accepted by the States as valid extension of customary international law of sea and did not seem to require any special justification for the innovations in the traditional law of sea. As such for giving legal uniformity and validity, the General Assembly in 1956 convened the United Nations Conference on the Law of Sea.[20] About 85 States attended the Conference at Geneva.[21] It had before it the four Draft Conventions that were prepared by the International Law Commission and were approved for consideration by the General Assembly. After thorough discussion, the Conference by a two-thirds majority adopted the four Conventions, and these were made open for ratification by States. These historic four Geneva Conventions on the Law of Sea incorporate all practical aspects of the developments as well as possible solutions for the raised problems of the time. It is observed that while the first of the following four conventions is basic, the other three conventions are in the nature of exceptions to the general or basic regime of the law of sea:

(1) The Convention on High Seas;[22]

(2) The Convention on the Territorial Sea and Contiguous Zones;[23]

(3) The Convention on Fishing and Conservation of the Living Resources of the High Seas;[24] and

(4) The Convention on Continental Shelf.[25]

08B. Though the 1982 Treaty Convention on the Law of Sea has come into force since 1993, yet these four 1958 Geneva Conventions continue to have more than academic or historic value. Since the 1982 Convention has been ratified till now, by only 141 States out of 191 members of the UNO.

09. *The 1958 Geneva Convention on High Seas*: This happens to be the first full codification of the law of sea, which is 'generally declaratory of established principles of international law'[26] as its preamble asserted. The term 'high seas' is defined (Article 1) relatively as "all parts of the seas not included in the territorial or internal waters of a State". No State "can validly purport to subject any part of them to its sovereignty" and the right to use the high seas is to be enjoyed equally with "reasonable regards to the interests of other States" both by coastal and non-coastal States of the world; and Article 2 further enumerates the freedoms of the States on high sea *viz.*, (i) freedom of navigation and flights; (ii) freedom to lay submarine cables and pipelines and (iii) freedom of fishing.[27]

(i) The freedom of navigation is made available both to coastal and non-coastal States. The landlocked States have a right of free access and transit to high seas through the territorial waters of coastal States as may be necessary to the ships flying the flag of such a landlocked State. This freedom is also made available to the intergovernmental organizations, like the UNO which can also be flag State. The principle of sovereign immunity applies only to warships and ships engaged only on 'governmental non-commercial service' in the sense that only the flag State has jurisdiction over them.[28] The Convention gives a legal status to the International Maritime Consultative Organization (IMCO)[29] for framing international codes and standards in the matters of 'safety at sea' and Article 10 enjoins the States to follow the rules which may be prescribed by the IMCO from time to time for navigation on high seas. Article 11 modifies the rule laid down by the Permanent Court of International Justice in the *Case of Lotus*[30] in the matters of collision in the ships of different nationality on the high sea. Now, only the flag State of the ship or the State of which the negligent or erring persons are nationals are to have jurisdiction to punish them to the exclusion of other interested States. Another old time crime, piracy on high sea is declared to be international crime, both for the act of piracy taking place on ships sailing or aircraft flying over the sea.[31] The Convention elaborately defines the right of 'hot pursuit' of the coastal States with regard to a fleeing foreign ship after violations of laws and regulations of the coastal State. 'Good reason' for violations and moving away after receiving visual or auditory signals are necessary conditions of 'hot pursuit'. This right starts when the ship is within territorial water or contiguous zone of a State and it comes to an end after the ship enters the territorial waters of its own country or of a third State. Hot pursuit has to be a continuous one-time operation. Only warships or specially authorized ships can make this 'hot pursuit' for this purpose. Similar is the position of aircraft of which 'hot pursuit' is made by a military aircraft of the coastal State. When 'hot pursuit' is unjustified, compensation must be made for any loss or damage suffered by the victim of 'hot pursuit'. The convention creates or gives recognition to the obligations of States also. The masters of ships are under a duty to protect the persons whose lives are in danger at sea, render help when a distress call is received from another ship or protect persons struggling against slave traffic. The Convention makes it obligatory for every State to take 'measures to prevent pollution of seas from dumping of radioactive waste' or oil discharges from ships and to protect submarine cables and pipelines[32] and to join or honour Conventions on prevention and control of pollution.[33]

(ii) *High Seas: Freedom relating to laying of Submarine Cables and Pipelines*: This freedom on high seas was regulated by a multilateral treaty for the first time by the 'Paris Convention on the Protection of Submarine Cables'[34] in 1884. It is made part of the freedom of high seas as a general international law by Articles 26 to 29 of the 1958 Convention on High Seas, that is, the right is now available to all States irrespective of the Paris Convention of 1884. The importance of this concept lies in the legal position that the States claiming contiguous zones, continental shelf and exclusive economic zone, have to honour and maintain this right of other States when the cables or pipelines pass through these. For any injury or breaking of cables or pipeline the responsible State has to pay compensation.

10. *The 1958 Convention on the Territorial Sea and Contiguous Zones*: "That the territorial jurisdiction of a State should extend beyond the low-water mark along its coast seemed to early writers on international law logical necessity of self-defense. At the same time it formed the rational basis of a claim to the exclusive enjoyment of local fisheries and other similar advantages."[35] The notion developed with effective control over the seaward area, the canon shot rule, and different States claimed different marginal sea as their territorial waters. In eighteenth century, Great Britain and USA claimed 3 miles, Sweden and Norway 4 miles, Spain and Portugal 6 miles, Mexico 9 miles and Russia 12 miles of coastal sea as their marginal, marine league or territorial sea for exclusive land-like jurisdiction. Later, for limited purpose of preventing smuggling of cargo and 'rum-running' the European States and the USA claimed additional sea limit against hovering vessels, now termed as contiguous zone.

10A. The Geneva Convention on Territorial Waters was first of the four conventions adopted in 1958, it codified much of the existing law and State practices but called itself an agreement and not a general international law. Its Part I does not define territorial waters directly, for lack of 2/3 majority at the Conference Article 1 simply states that the 'sovereignty of a State extends, beyond its land territory and its internal waters, to a belt of sea adjacent to its coast described as territorial sea'. The consensus of States was that the limit of territorial sea could be 3, 6 or 12 miles only and not any other figure. Not satisfied, after the Convention was adopted, some States particularly the Latin American States laid claim to 50 or even 200 miles as their territorial waters limit. However, the international opinion has not favoured such extensive claims. The International Court of Justice has held that a unilateral fixation of territorial sea limit has no legal validity; other States concerned must recognize it.[36] Earlier International Court of Justice had in 1951 held that a unilateral extension of territorial sea limit beyond 12 nautical miles would not be binding on other States as such.[37] Next, the question was from where the width of territorial sea is to be delimited or fixed and monitored. The Convention recognized the base-line method, but where this method was not possible the Convention allowed the existing method of low tide watermark point.[38] The Convention significantly ensured 'innocent passage to all ships in territorial States without need of prior permission'. This innocent passage included navigation, stoppage, anchoring but that not being 'prejudicial to the peace, good order or security of the coastal State'. In the territorial waters the foreign fishing vessels have to observe published laws and regulations for preventing of fishing in such waters, and the foreign submarines have to navigate on the surface and show their flags (Article 12). The Convention followed the customary international law in the matters of exercise of jurisdiction by the coastal State on foreign merchant ships, warships and other State owned ships other than warships (Articles 18-23).

10B. Part II of the Convention provided for a contiguous zone of 12 miles from the base line from which the width of territorial water is measured.[39] The purpose of this contiguous zone was to enable the coastal State to exercise control that might be necessary for preventing infringements of customs, fiscal, immigration or sanitary regulations taking place within its territory or territorial waters. The contiguous zone was coextensive with the territorial sea. Therefore, for those States that had opted for 12 miles for their territorial sea, this contiguous zone was meaningless. However, this defect has been removed by the UNCLOS III by Article 33 of the Informal Composite Negotiating Text (ICNT) by recognizing a uniform 24 nautical miles wide contiguous zone for all coastal States. Proceeding under this, India has also since 1976 claimed a contiguous zone by the Maritime Zones Act.

11. *The Convention on Fishing and Conservation of the Living Resources of the High Seas*: This third of 1958 Conventions gave a universal recognition of equality of States to exploit the fisheries and living resources of the high seas and to adopt measures for their conservation against depletion. It incorporates the contents of the second proclamation made by

the USA in 1945. It provided a uniform basis for regulation of mutual interests of interested States in the high seas and to the preferential claims and rights in this regard of the adjacent coastal States. It is to be remembered that since 1950s the practice of long-distance fishing with factory ships had started and States could send their fishing ships thousands of miles away from their coast in the high seas in areas that were adjacent to other coastal States. The States could make special agreements for regulating fishing in common interest by involving the Food and Agriculture Organization (FAO) in the process. Disputed issues could be submitted to special commission established by the States concerned and also ultimately to the International Court of Justice.[40]

12. *The Convention on Continental Shelf*: This Convention gave the seal of legality of international law to thc doctrine of exclusive claims of coastal States to exploit minerals including oil from the submarine areas coming under the definition of continental shelf. Article 1 gave a much extended content to continental shelf when it defined it as referring to:

"(a) The seabed and submarine areas adjacent to the coast but outside the area of the territorial sea, to a depth of 200 metres, or beyond that limit, to where the depth of the superjacent waters admit of the exploitation of the natural resources of the said areas;

(b) The seabed and the subsoil of similar submarine areas adjacent to the coasts of the islands."

The Convention came to be known for (i) converting exploitation of sea for minerals by exploitation of natural resources, (ii) the incorporation of exploitable capacity of States in addition to the depth of 200 metres, and (iii) for extending the concept of continental shelf to all islands of a State. Further, the Convention clarified that the coastal State would have 'sovereign rights' over the natural resources of the seabed and subsoil including minerals and not just a preferential or regulatory right. The sovereign rights are exclusive in nature and do not depend on effective or notional occupation by the State of those areas and there need not be any proclamation to that effect.[41] The Convention protected the freedoms of the high seas over the areas to be included in the continental shelf by various coastal States and laid down the basic conditions for harmonizing the freedom of high seas with the new developments that were likely to take shape as a result of the provisions of its Articles 3, 4 and 5.

Consequential Developments of the Four 1958 Conventions

13. The causes for the thorough revision of the law of sea as developed and evolved by the four 1958 Conventions, by the fresh 1982 Treaty on Law of Sea, lay in the consequences of these Conventions and the all-round technological advancements pertaining to the exploitation of sea or using it for one or the other purpose. All the four Conventions had provided for their revision after the expiration of five years from the date from which these would enter into force. A contracting party could make the request for such a revision at anytime. This request could be made by means of a notification in writing addressed to the Secretary General of the UNO. Thereafter it was for the General Assembly of the UNO to decide what steps, if any, were to be taken in that matter of revision.

14. *Problems Left Unsolved or Generated by the 1958 Conventions*: The four 1958 Conventions rather materially and progressively[42] codified much of the existing customary law relating to the sea in the common interests of the coastal States. Such States were in majority and were concerned States. Landlocked States were treated as generally unconcerned States. The concerned States appropriated for their benefit the undefined limits on the high seas adjacent to their coast when the 'high sea' was defined as "all parts of the sea that are not included in the territorial sea or internal waters of a State", and this had the element of fluidity. At the same time the width of territorial sea and continental shelf were left undefined. Further, the Conventions differed the rights of developed and undeveloped States both in the definition of continental shelf and the contiguous zones for the control and regulation of fisheries, which depended upon specialized scientific knowledge and exploitability skills. The underdeveloped of the coastal States were more interested in keeping off the exploitation of their continental shelf by other better technologically accomplished

and equipped States. As such several disputes regarding the demarcation of continental shelf[43] and contiguous zones of conflicting claims arose, particularly where the seas, such as, North Sea, were shallow. Around 1970, it was apparent that a further development in the law of sea to harmonize the diversity of claims and to make the definitions precise under various 1958 Conventions was imperative.[44]

15. *Undeveloped States and Deep Sea*: After the Second World War, there was the question of reconstruction of devastated Europe, this process continued till late 1950s. After that in 1960s there was a scramble among the developed or industrialized States to capture the consumer markets of new States. At this stage it was found that it was necessary to increase or develop the purchasing power of poor States or unindustrialized new States. There was a concerted effort in this direction during 1960s resulting in various ideas for raising the gross national product (GNP) of the States world over so that the purchasing power of people may increase for the benefit of industrialized States. The once active United Nations Conference on Trade and Development (UNCTAD) was a result of this process. However, the undeveloped States in this process became conscious of their 'right to development' as a human right and consequential obligation of rich developed States to help them, leading to the United Nations Development Programme (UNDP). This had effect on the development of law of sea for the benefit of undeveloped States. The exploitation of mineral or natural resources in continental shelf and contiguous zones had become a part of international law, but the riches of deep sea in fact and in law still belonged to every State and humanity in general.[45]

16. *Humanitarian Use of Sea Wealth*: The representative of Malta in General Assembly session of 1967 moved a proposal for deep sea exploitation internationally, to be done under the authority of United Nations. The fabulous wealth of the oceans was to be utilized for making the international organizations more purposeful and effective with sea wealth generated finances, and for giving facelift to the people particularly of the undeveloped States. The proposal was backed by the majority of the members of General Assembly as against few developed

States. After some spadework on the "question of reservation exclusively for peaceful purposes of the seabed and ocean floor and the subsoil thereof underlying the high seas beyond the limits of national jurisdiction, and the uses of these resources in the interests of mankind, the General Assembly in December 1968 constituted[46] a Committee to go ahead with the task of preparing the groundwork for international regime for exploitation of seabed resources. There was confusion on the demarcation between jurisdictions on continental shelf and high sea under the 1958 Conventions and the members of General Assembly pointed this out. Thereafter it was opined that there was a genuine need to make the matter 'clear and precise'. Next year, 1969, the General Assembly adopted a number of resolutions: (i) That there was no clear demarcation between the sea within and beyond the jurisdiction of a State and it expressed the desirability to call a Conference on the Law of the Sea for resolving the issues[47], (ii) that it was desirable to constitute an international regime for the areas falling beyond national jurisdiction of a State[48], (iii) that the outer limits of national jurisdiction in high seas were legally a fluid proposition which had to be clarified and made precise. As such "pending establishment of aforementioned intentional regime (under resolution 2574D):

(a) States and persons physical and juridical are bound to refrain from all activities of exploitation of the resources of the area of seabed and ocean floor, and the subsoil thereof beyond the limits of national jurisdiction; and

(b) No claim to any part of that area or its resources shall be recognized".[49]

This 'prohibitory transitory' step taken by the General Assembly was highly significant and was in favour of undeveloped States. Since most of the 'developed' States have not fully acceded to the subsequent 1982 Law of Sea Treaty, the above prohibition continues to remain in order and operative as part of international law and as appendage to the 1958 Conventions on High Seas.

16A. The General Assembly moved ahead on the above proposition and resolved on the establishment in immediate future of appropriate international regime for exploration and exploitation of high seas beyond the limits of national jurisdiction. It made a highly significant formal 'Declaration of Principles' by which the seabed and its natural resources were to be common heritage of mankind and could not be appropriated by the States. The exploration and exploitation of the resources of seabed and ocean-floor and their subsoil was to be done under an international regime, and the profits were to be utilized for the mankind as a whole irrespective of national boundaries. The Declaration of Principles[50] is worth noting since it continues to be an integral part of the law of sea. It provided that:

"(1) The seabed and ocean-floor and the subsoil thereof, beyond the limits of national jurisdiction (hereinafter referred to as areas) as well as the resources of the areas are common heritage of mankind.

(2) The area shall not be subject to appropriation by any means by States or persons, natural or judicial, and that no State shall claim or exercise sovereignty or sovereign rights over any part thereof."

Third UN Conference on Law of the Sea (UNCLOS III)

17. The UN General Assembly adopted[51] an important resolution in 1970 under which it called a third United Nations Conference on the Law of Sea (UNCLOS) to be held in 1973. The assigned tasks of UNCLOS III were: (a) to define international seabed, (b) to formulate a regime for high seas, continental shelf and territorial sea, etc. This was third Conference under the provisions for revision of the 1958 four Conventions. This Conference had the mandate of General Assembly to review and revise the whole of the accomplishments of the four 1958 Conventions by taking into account the difficulties experienced, gaps left unprovided for and the latest developments on the ideas for exploration and exploitation of seabed and ocean floors, set into motion by the proposals of Malta since 1967 and legally identified by the General Assembly in 'Declaration of Principles' in 1970.

18. *Background Documents for UNCLOS III*: The

UNCLOS III had for its deliberations the four 1958 Geneva Conventions on Law of Sea and the proposals by the two sub-committees[52] of the Committees on Seabed and Ocean-floor beyond the Limits of National Jurisdiction[53] which was established by the General Assembly in 1970. Further, the detailed grievances of States, problems felt since 1958 and needs for future had been already highlighted by the General Assembly for study and deliberation.[54] This had been supplemented by the Report (1972) submitted[55] by UN Secretary General also on the problems, issues and needs of landlocked States for making appropriate changes in the law of sea.

19. *Sessions of UNCLOS III*: The Conference was convened in New York in 1973 where in December 1973, the UNCLOS III held its first conference. Its task ended nine years later along with the adoption in 1982 of the United Nations Convention on the Law of the Sea. During those nine years, representatives of States moved back and forth between New York and Geneva, holding marathon negotiations that produced the Convention. Three committees were appointed which by themselves narrate the parametres of the tasks ahead: The Committee I was to prepare treaty articles on 'Seabed and Ocean-floor Beyond the Limits of National Jurisdiction' and related matters; Committee II was to lay down articles dealing with maritime zones, claims of landlocked States on sea and other preferential rights, and Committee III was to deal with treaty articles on marine environment, scientific research and transfer of technology from developed States to poor States on related matters. The second session of UNCLOS III was held at Caracas in 1974 in which general discussions were held on the problems and a decision was taken on the procedure to be adopted in the meetings for reaching on agreements and how the disagreements were to be resolved both in the Committees and in the plenary sessions.[56] It was agreed that on those points on which agreement was reached in plenary session, the agreement should hold good forthwith. Only those points on which no decision were taken would be further deliberated upon for solution in the Committees. The sessions of UNCLOS III were marked with organized bargaining between the majority composed of

underdeveloped States and the minority composed of high technology States but both sides wanted a settled law of sea. The scientifically advanced States had done a thorough survey of the earth's crust by satellites technology and underwater investigations and wanted to extract as much jurisdiction over the sea as may be possible. For them it was a kind of underwater 'gold rush' and instead of long drawn negotiation the industrial powers were willing to make beneficial compromises. Depending on their future acquisition of technology, most of the coastal States also cautiously acquiesced in the demands made by the advanced States.

19A. The third session of UNCLOS III, 1975, led to the conclusion that the issues before the three committees were quite interrelated and a 'Single Negotiating Text' was proposed which contained the minimum for discussion at the next sessions of the Conference. The fourth and fifth sessions of Conference, 1976, led to the formation of 'Revised Single Negotiating Text'. The seventh session of Conference, 1977, produced the 'Informal Composite Negotiating Text' (ICNT) for a Convention on law of sea, which recognized a 200 nautical miles of Exclusive Economic Zone (EEZ). The seventh (1978) and eighth (1979) sessions recognized for coastal States a 350 nautical miles wide outer maximum limit for continental shelf and some additional qualified mining rights outside the EEZ. In 1980, the ninth session, completed the remaining task of defining the composition and voting pattern, etc., in the International Seabed Authority (Part XI of the 1982 Convention) for exploration and exploitation of deep-sea.

19B. The final version of ICNT that emerged after the last or the ninth session of 1980, showed a number of compromises between the majority of undeveloped and poor coastal States and landlocked States on one hand, and the scientifically highly developed hi-tech States who had with their penetrating data collection equipments made thorough survey of earth's crust by satellites technology, underwater investigations and otherwise, on the other. Former depended upon the 'Declaration of Principles' made by the General Assembly[57] for safeguarding their interests if no agreements were reached. Under the compromises reached ultimately both sides got the EEZ, while the industrialized States or their industrial corporations in addition obtained the opportunity of getting mining rights or contracts in the EEZ of less developed States and also in the 'Area' of the high seas beyond the limits of EEZ, for which there were to be few competitors. Powerful States in addition to sea-wealth were very much interested in their freedom of navigation which enabled them to reach the coast beyond territorial waters of their enemy States. They succeeded in restricted definitions of territorial sea, bays and sea straits. Since the procedure adopted was that when agreement on any point was reached in any session of the plenary meeting of UNCLOS III, it became final, the States developed the practice of perfecting their sea claims as and when decisions were reached without waiting for the final treaty. The major industrialized States have not cared to formally accede to the Treaty on Law of Sea, 1982, since the Treaty is now an established legal regime for the sea and these States have already appropriated all benefits generously made available to the coastal States. The concepts of archipelagos status, continental shelf for islands, the exclusive economic zones for coastal States, the rules for transit and innocent passage through straits and gulfs, the rights of landlocked states and the recognition and establishment of International Seabed Authority are some of the innovative achievements of the Treaty. These benefits arising out of these new features are available equally to the developed and undeveloped coastal States. The Convention was to be adopted as a "Package deal", that is, to be accepted as a whole, in all its parts and without reservation on any aspect. The Convention carries the undertaking by the adherent Governments not to take any action that might defeat its objects and purposes. Ratification of or accession to the Convention implies the consent of a State to be bound by its entire provisions. The Convention came into force on 16th November 1994, one year after Guyana joined the Treaty as its 60th Party in accordance with its Article 308 (1). The Convention has 17 Parts and 320 Articles along with nine annexes and four resolutions[58] adopted by the Conference to complete its Final Act which is its Part XVII. The International Organization can also accede to the 1982 Convention under the conditions laid down by its Part XVI. The high sea or ocean has been pushed away from the coast and the former exceptions to it, continental shelf and EEZ, are now mainstay of the Treaty.

20. As mentioned, the Convention on Law of Sea of 1982, formally a Treaty, is an unprecedented attempt by the international community to regulate all aspects of the so far fragmented laws of the sea, of the resources of the sea and the uses of the ocean by one Convention framed under the patronage and approval of the General Assembly of the United Nations Organization, and thus to bring a stable legal order or a functional regime of the sea by the Law of Sea Convention. The Convention works on the premise that the problems of ocean space are closely interrelated and need to be considered as a whole. The Preamble records 'the desire to settle, in a spirit of mutual understanding and cooperation, all issues relating to the law of the sea' and regards the Treaty to be of historic significance 'as an important contribution to the maintenance of peace, justice and progress for all peoples of the world. It recognized the 'desirability of establishing through this Convention, with due regard for the sovereignty of all States, a legal order for the seas and oceans which will facilitate international communication, and will promote the peaceful uses of the seas and oceans, the equitable and efficient utilization of their resources, the conservation of their living resources, and the study, protection and preservation of the marine environment'. It further emphasized that 'the achievement of these goals will contribute to the realization of a just and equitable international economic order which takes into account the interests and needs of mankind as a whole and, in particular, the special interests and needs of developing countries, whether coastal or landlocked'. It also noted that 'the codification and progressive development of the law of the sea achieved in this Convention will contribute to the strengthening of peace, security, cooperation and friendly relations among all nations in conformity with the principles of justice and equal rights and will promote the economic and social advancement of all peoples of the world, in accordance with the Purposes and Principles of the United Nations as set forth in the Charter'. The Preamble accepted that the Treaty

was a continuous process and had its background in the developments since the United Nations Conferences on the Law of the Sea held at Geneva in 1958 and 1960 while the later developments have 'accentuated the need for a new and generally acceptable Convention on the law of the sea'. The Preamble also recorded that the UNCLOS III was constrained to develop the principles embodied in resolution 2749 (XXV) of 17 December 1970. In this Resolution, the General Assembly of the United Nations solemnly declared *inter alia* 'that the area of the seabed and ocean floor and the subsoil thereof, beyond the limits of national jurisdiction, as well as its resources, are the common heritage of mankind, the exploration and exploitation of which shall be carried out for the benefit of mankind as a whole, irrespective of the geographical location of States'.

21. The 1982 Treaty or Convention on Law of Sea by its Part I gives some basic definitions particularly with reference to the Seabed Authority, pollution of marine environment, dumping and those entities which can be Parties to the Treaty. Most of these concepts were not pronounced part of the customary law of sea.

22. The Part II of the Convention deals with a precise and detailed regime for Territorial Sea and Contiguous Zones. Making a change in the 1958 Convention, Article 3 of the Treaty provides territorial sea upto a limit not exceeding 12 nautical miles measured from the baseline determined in accordance[59] with this Convention. Article 33 fixes the breadth of Contiguous Zone at '24 nautical miles from the baseline from which the breadth of the territorial sea is measured' giving to the coastal State the control necessary to (a) prevent infringement of its customs, fiscal, immigration or sanitary laws and regulations• within its territory or territorial sea and (b) punish infringement of the above laws and regulations committed within its territory or territorial sea.

22A. The determination of baseline has been a matter of controversy and diverse claims had been made by the adjacent States or States situated in bays and gulfs. Now fixed and uniform principles have been evolved by the 1982 Convention. It provides normal baseline for measuring the breadth of the territorial sea that is the low-water line along the coast as marked on large-scale charts officially recognized by the coastal State. In the case of 'Reefs' the baseline for measuring the breadth of the territorial sea is the seaward low-water line of the reef, as shown by the appropriate symbol on charts officially recognized by the coastal State. It is further defined that: (i) In localities where the coastline is deeply indented and cut into, or if there is a fringe of islands along the coast in its immediate vicinity, the method of straight baselines joining appropriate points may be employed in drawing the baseline from which the breadth of the territorial sea is measured. (ii) Where because of the presence of a delta and other natural conditions the coastline is highly unstable, the appropriate points may be selected along the furthest seaward extent of the low-water line and, notwithstanding subsequent regression of the low-water line, the straight baselines shall remain effective until changed by the coastal State in accordance with this Convention. The breadth of the 'bays' has also been increased from the existing 6 nautical miles. Now, the waters enclosed in a bay measuring upto 24 nautical miles from the low watermark of the natural entrance points of the bay will be internal waters of the States.[60]

22B. Marking of the baseline for territorial waters has been a controversial matter. In cases where the coastline is continuous, the mean low tide mark has been the normal method for demarcation. Where the coastline is studded with islands the line joining appropriate protruding points forms the baseline for measuring territorial waters breadth. The International Court of Justice upheld[61] the method of defining baseline by straight lines adopted by Norway for about 1000 miles of its seacoast by joining 48 outermost points of rock-ramparts as appropriate points on the islands in continuity as 'dictated by geographical realities'.

23. The legal status of the territorial sea, of the air space over the territorial sea and of its bed and subsoil remains unchanged. The Convention recognizes[62] that the sovereignty of a coastal State (i) extends, beyond its land territory and internal waters and, in the case of an archipelagic State, its archipelagic waters, to an adjacent belt of sea, described as the

territorial sea, (ii) extends to the air space over the territorial sea as well as to its bed and subsoil, and (iii) extending over the territorial sea is exercised subject to this Convention and to other rules of international law. Accordingly, subject to this Convention, ships of all States, whether coastal or landlocked, enjoy the right of innocent passage through the territorial sea.[63] The 'passage' means[64] navigation through the territorial sea for the purpose of (a) traversing that sea without entering internal waters or calling at a roadstead or port facility outside internal waters; or (b) proceeding to or from internal waters or a call at such roadstead or port facility. 'The passage has to be continuous and expeditious. However, passage includes stopping and anchoring, but only in so far as the same are incidental to ordinary navigation or are rendered necessary by force *majeure* or distress or for the purpose of rendering assistance to persons, ships or aircrafts in danger or distress'. At the same time, 'innocent passage' carries with it the obligation[65] that it should not be 'prejudicial to the peace, good order or security of the coastal State and such passage shall take place in conformity with this Convention and with other rules of international law. Article 19 (2) visualizes twelve conditions when the passage shall not be innocent and will be, therefore, illegal. The coastal State has regulatory powers over the traffic in the territorial waters which should be given due publicity.[66] The powers are to be exercised (i) the safety of navigation and the regulation of maritime traffic; (ii) the protection of cables and pipelines; (iii) the prevention of infringement of the fisheries laws and regulations of the coastal State; (iv) the preservation of the environment of the coastal State; (v) the prevention, reduction and control of pollution; or (vi) the prevention of infringement of the customs, fiscal, immigration or sanitary laws and regulations of the coastal State, among other matters. Further, in the territorial sea, submarines and other underwater vehicles are required to navigate on the surface and to show their flag.[67] Foreign nuclear-powered ships and ships carrying nuclear or other inherently dangerous or noxious substances, when exercising the right of innocent passage through the territorial sea, are to carry documents and observe special precautionary measures established for such ships by international agreements.[68] The customary international law on the exercise of jurisdiction by the coastal State in territorial waters, inland waters or straits has been elaborately codified,[69] viz., the extent of jurisdiction on (a) foreign ships operated for commercial purposes, (b) warships and other government ships operated for non-commercial purposes; or the duties and rights of the coastal State.[70]

24. *Straits used for International Navigation*: The 1982 Treaty by its Part III introduces a law for freedom of innocent navigation through international straits, that is narrow sea connecting oceans or sea on the two sides. The straits are traditionally recognized international waterways that have been used for international navigation between one part of the high seas or an exclusive economic zone and another part of the high seas or an exclusive economic zone.[71] The need for this separate provision for straits arose since the uniform 12-mile territorial sea and 24 nautical miles bays limit under Part II now places under national jurisdiction of coastal States strategic passages, particularly such as, Strait of Gibraltar which is only 8 nautical miles wide access to the Mediterranean sea from Atlantic ocean, the 20 nautical miles wide Strait of Malacca which forms main sea route between the Pacific and Indian Oceans, 21 nautical miles wide Strait of Hormuz that provides navigational passage to the oil-producing areas of the Gulf[72], and Bab el Mandeb, a 14 nautical miles wide link connecting the Indian Ocean with the Red Sea. For military, commercial and strategic reasons such straits became sensitive matters and the most of the States wanted to retain their international water passage rights in such waterways before these accepted 12 nautical miles limit for territorial waters and 24 nautical miles limit for bays instead of 3 or 6 nautical miles.

24A. The coastal States exercise their sovereignty over internationally recognized straits 'subject to this Part and to other rules of international law'.[73] Particularly, nothing in this Part III is to affect (a) any areas of internal waters within a strait, except where the establishment of a straight baseline in accordance with the method set forth in article 7 has the effect of enclosing as internal waters areas which had not previously been considered as such; (b) the legal status of the waters beyond the territorial seas of States bordering straits as exclusive economic zones or high seas; or (c) the legal regime in straits in which passage is regulated in whole or in part by long-standing international conventions in force specifically relating to such straits.[74] Further, this 'Part is not to apply to a strait used for international navigation if there exists through the strait a route through the high seas or through an exclusive economic zone of similar convenience with respect to navigational and hydrographical characteristics; in such routes, the other relevant Parts of this Convention, including the provisions regarding the freedoms of navigation and overflight, apply'.[75] Then there are those straits that are used for international navigation between one part of the high seas or an exclusive economic zone and another part of the high seas or an exclusive economic zone. In such straits, all ships and aircrafts enjoy the 'right of transit passage', which is not to be impeded; except that, if the strait is formed by an island of a State bordering the strait and its mainland, transit passage shall not apply if there exists seaward of the island a route through the high seas or through an exclusive economic zone of similar convenience with respect to navigational and hydrographical characteristics. Transit passage means the exercise in accordance with this Part of the freedom of navigation and overflight solely for the purpose of 'continuous and expeditious' transit of the strait between one part of the high seas or an exclusive economic zone and another part of the high seas or an exclusive economic zone.[76] The right of transit is to be exercised according to international regulations, procedures and practices as laid down in the Part itself while the coastal States have to be non-discriminatory and this right of other States cannot be obstructed or suspended by the coastal States. The right of transit passage has at all times to be 'innocent' passage as defined in Article 19 of the Treaty.[77]

25. *Archipelagic States*: The 1982 Treaty on the Law of Sea recognizes new juridical status of archipelagic States with archipelagic waters and archipelagic air space over the sea enclosed as internal waters.[78] The archipelagic waters of a State exist along with exclusive jurisdiction just as on territorial sea, on seabed of such internal waters. Geographically, in nature

the archipelagos[79] is a group of islands closely situated forming an intrinsic economic and political entity, *e.g.* Indonesia,[80] Philippines or Canada are archipelagic nations. The boundaries of archipelagic State are as may be determined by drawing straight archipelagic baselines joining the outermost points of the outermost islands and drying reefs of the archipelago, provided that within such baselines are included the main islands and an area in which the ratio of the area of the water to the area of the land, including atolls, is between 1 to 1 and 9 to 1. Further, the length of such baselines is not to exceed 100 nautical miles, but only up to 3 per cent of the total number of baselines enclosing any archipelago, may exceed 100 nautical miles up to a maximum length of 125 nautical miles.

25A. The advantage of archipelagic status is that all the sea falling within the encirclement of archipelagic baselines becomes the internal water of such an archipelagic State. Further, the sovereignty of an archipelagic State extends to the archipelagic waters enclosed by the archipelagic baselines drawn in accordance with article 47, regardless of their depth or distance from the coast. This sovereignty extends to the air space over the archipelagic waters, seabed and subsoil thereof, and the natural resources contained therein irrespective of sea lanes that continue for other States.[81] Bilateral existing agreements for fishing and other legitimate activities including those relating to submarine cables in the waters, now becoming internal waters as a result of archipelagic status shall continue. The ships of all States enjoy the right of innocent passage through the demarcated and published water lanes in the archipelagic waters, in accordance with Part II, section 3.[82]

26. *Exclusive Economic Zone (EEZ)*: It has been made an important zone of rights on sea for the States by Part V of the 1982 Convention on Law of Sea and constitutes a stable development for the economic benefit of the coastal States[83]. It is a compromise between the changing concept of high seas, doctrine of continental shelf, the claim for exclusive fishing zones by the States and the fishing conservation zones claimed by different States from time to time. International Court of Justice had also prior to the conclusion of the Treaty, recognized

the legitimacy of the concern of the coastal States for developing fisheries in exclusively defined conservation zones.[84] Now, only those States, which have not acceded to the 1982 Treaty, have made separate proclamations claiming Exclusive Fishery Zones (EFZ), while the members of the Treaty have only to announce regulatory steps in their EEZ since the Treaty itself grants EEZ to them. Under the Treaty EEZ is the coastal sea area beyond and adjacent to the territorial sea upto a maximum breadth of 200 nautical miles from the baseline from which the breadth of the territorial sea is measured. Beyond EEZ lies the high sea that is regulated by Part VIII of the Treaty. Where the delimitation of EEZ by different adjacent or oppositely situated States overlap, the solution has to be found by agreement on the basis of international law, for achieving an 'equitable solution' but where the States fail, they shall take resource to the settlement procedures provided by the Treaty itself by its Part XV.

26A. Article 56 of the 1982 Convention provides that in the EEZ the coastal State has (a) the sovereign rights for (i) exploring and exploiting, conserving and managing living and non-living resources of the seabed, subsoil and superadjacent waters, (ii) other economic activities in the zone directed for exploitation and exploration for production of energy water, currents and winds; (b) jurisdiction subject to relevant provisions of the Convention for (i) establishment and use of artificial islands, installations and structures, (ii) marine scientific research, and (iii) preservation of marine environment; and, (c) other rights and duties, as provided for in the Convention. With regard to other States of the world, the rights and duties in the EEZ of a State defined in Article 58 are only three out of the six freedoms of the high seas generally made available to the States by Article 87, *viz.*, (a) freedom of navigation, (b) freedom of overflight, (c) freedom to lay submarine cables and pipelines. Other pertinent rules for the regime in high seas contained in Articles 88 to 115 apply in the EEZ of a State to the extent such rights are not incompatible with the new regime for EEZ laid down by the Part V. The important thing is that now there is no absolute freedom to fish for other State in the EEZ of a member State of the Treaty Convention. A coastal State whose economy is overwhelmingly dependent on exploitation of the living resources of the EEZ is not obliged to share the harvest with other States.[85] The coastal State is to decide its capacity to harvest the living resources of the EEZ. The harvest that is in excess of its capacity is to be allotted by the coastal State to other States 'through agreements or other arrangements' retaining to itself the regulatory and compensatory rights in the interests of the conservation of fisheries. While giving access to other States to fish, the coastal State is entitled to take into account all relevant factors, such as national interests, requirements of the developing, landlocked or 'geographically disadvantaged' countries of the region, and the need to minimize economic dislocation to other States 'whose nationals have habitually fished in the zones or which have made substantial efforts in the research and identification of fishery stocks'.[86] The permitted other States are to comply with conservation measures and with other norms, terms and conditions established by the published regulations of the coastal State.

27. *The Continental Shelf*: The continental shelf is by far the most productive part of the adjacent sea for exploration and exploitation. As examined earlier, its conception has brought tremendous innovations in the law of sea since the 1950s. The Part VI of the 1982 Convention in general retains the provisions relating to the regime of continental shelf as laid down by the fourth Geneva Convention of 1958 with much extended rights for the coastal State and with resulting obligations also. The definition of continental shelf has been made more precise by dropping depth and exploitability phrases. It now contains the seabed and subsoil of the submarine areas (i) that extend beyond its territorial sea throughout the natural prolongation of its land territory to the outer edge of the continental margin, or (ii) to a distance of 200 nautical miles from the baselines from which the breadth of the territorial sea is measured in situations where the outer edge of the continental margin does not extend up to that distance. The 'continental margin' itself comprises of the submerged prolongation of the landmass of the coastal State, and consists of the seabed and subsoil of the shelf, the slope and the rise. It does not include the deep ocean floor with its

oceanic ridges or the subsoil thereof. However, whatever methods are chosen by the coastal State for delimiting the boundaries of continental shelf, the outer limit of the continental shelf shall not exceed 350 nautical miles from the baselines from which the breadth of the territorial sea is measured. The rider is that wherever the continental shelf extends beyond 200 nautical miles of the EEZ, the coastal State is under an obligation to make payments and contributions annually to the International Seabed Authority on their production from non-living resources beyond the EEZ but from its continental shelf. The payments shall start after five years from the date production starts at the rate of one per cent of the value of production at the site and shall reach upto a maximum of five per cent.[87] Unlike the situation earlier, for exercising such rights in the continental shelf there is no need for formal occupation or proclamation to that effect for excluding other States from this area, and the rights extend both over the living and the non-living resources of the seabed and subsoil.[88] In general, the rights of the coastal State for the exploration and exploitation of its continental shelf are exclusive and no other State can enter in it for this purpose, even in the sea beyond the EEZ but within 350 nautical miles outer limit of the continental shelf.

27A. Article 83 of the 1982 Convention provides for the delimitation of the continental shelf between States with opposite or adjacent coasts. This is to be done by agreement on the basis of international law as referred to in Article 38 of the Statute of the International Court of Justice, with the aim of achieving an equitable solution. This Article does not provide any equitable method along with the law recognized by International Court of Justice which is regarded as equitable rule of international law. While interpreting Article 6 (2) of 1958 Geneva Convention on Continental Shelf the International Court of Justice[89] had recognized the median or equidistance line methods as recommendatory since equitable situation for demarcation was to be achieved where there was no agreement. It had proceeded to define the method for equitable demarcation in absence of an agreement also. In view of the fact that Article 83 of the 1982 Convention prescribes equitable solution based on agreements, the median and equidistance methods as under Article 6 (2) of 1958 Convention have become non-binding, and the decision of the International Court of Justice shall be equitable rule of international law applicable to States when demarcation is not reached by the States of their continental shelf by agreement. In 1985, the ICJ looked[90] into Article 83 (1) of the 1982 Convention to say that it represented rules of customary international law and held that "the principles and rules, applicable to the delimitation of continental shelf area are those which are appropriate to bring about an equitable result".

27B. The rights of the coastal State over the continental shelf do not affect the legal status of the superjacent waters or of the air space above those waters. Also, the exercise of the rights of the coastal State over the continental shelf must not infringe or result in any unjustifiable interference with navigation and other rights and freedoms of other States as provided for in this Convention. All States are entitled to lay submarine cables and pipelines on the continental shelf, in accordance with the provisions of Article 79 of the 1982 Convention and the coastal State is not to impede the laying or maintenance of such cables or pipelines on the grounds of exploitation of natural resources or the prevention of pollution from pipelines. However, the delineation of the path or course for the laying of such pipelines on the continental shelf is subject to the consent of or rather consensus with the coastal State.[91] Article 60 of the 1982 Convention applies *mutatis mutandis* to artificial islands, installations and structures that can be raised by the States on their continental shelf. The coastal State shall have the exclusive right to authorize and regulate drilling on the continental shelf for all purposes.

28. *The High Seas*: The 1982 Convention has adopted a negative approach in defining and dealing with the 'High Seas'. Article 86 does not define high seas but mentions that the provisions of Part VII "apply to all parts of the sea that are not included in the exclusive economic zone, in the territorial sea or in the internal waters of a State, or in the archipelagic waters of an archipelagic State. It specifically states that this article 86 in dealing with application of Part VII does not entail any

abridgement of the freedoms enjoyed by all States in the exclusive economic zone in accordance with Article 58 of the 1982 Convention. In the matter of freedom the high seas are open to all States, whether coastal or landlocked. The freedom[92] of the high seas is to be exercised under the conditions laid down by this Convention and by other rules of international law. The freedoms of high seas (1) Comprise, *inter alia*, both for coastal and landlocked States:

(a) Freedom of navigation;

(b) Freedom of overflight;

(c) Freedom to lay submarine cables and pipelines, subject to Part VI;

(d) Freedom to construct artificial islands and other installations permitted under international law subject to Part VI;

(e) Freedom of fishing, subject to the conditions laid down in section 2;

(f) Freedom of scientific research, subject to Parts VI and XIII.

(2) These freedoms of high seas are to be exercised by all States with due regard for the interests of other States in their exercise of the freedom of the high seas, and also with due regard for the rights under this Convention with respect to activities in the 'Area' covered by Part XI of the Convention.

(3) The International Maritime Organization (IMO), a Specialized Agency of United Nations Organization regulates the rules regarding shipping including 'safety of life' at sea, in all of its phases. It has special reference however here to Article 94 of the 1982 Convention. The IMO came into effect in March 1958 as Inter-Governmental Maritime Consultative Organization and later as International Maritime Consultative Organization. It is responsible for framing international codes and standards in the matter of 'safety of life' at sea. The IMO is composed of (a) Assembly, (b) Council and (c) Secretariat. Its functions and purposes are: (i) to provide machinery for cooperation among governments in the field of governmental regulation and practice relating to technical matters, including those concerning safety

at sea; (ii) to encourage the removal of discriminatory action and all unnecessary restrictions on shipping by the governments; (iii) to consider matters concerning shipping that might be referred to it by any organ or specialized agency of the UN; and (iv) to provide for the exchange of information among governments on matters referred to it for consideration by governments. The States are enjoined by the 1982 Convention to follow the rules and regulations laid down by the IMO.

28A. The 1982 Convention discourages use of high seas for war purposes in that the 'high seas shall be reserved for peaceful purposes' only. Thus, the law of sea has been joined with the purposes of the United Nations. The high seas cannot be appropriated by any State and it has been specifically provided that "no State may validly purport to subject any part of the high seas to its sovereignty" and every State, whether coastal or landlocked, has the right to sail ships flying its flag on the high seas. The United Nations and its specialized agencies including International Atomic Energy Agency, for example, have been allowed to fly their flags on the ships sailing in the high seas. Every State must maintain a 'register of shipping' and these States exercise their jurisdiction and control in administrative, technical and social matters of the ship. The flag State exercises complete jurisdiction over internal law of the ship and has to ensure that the ship follows international standards as are necessary[93] to ensure safety at sea as laid down by IMO with regard, *inter alia*, to:

(a) The construction, equipment and seaworthiness of ships;
(b) The manning of ships, labour conditions and the training of crews, taking into account the applicable international instruments;
(c) The use of signals, the maintenance of communications and the prevention of collisions.

28B. The freedom of navigation on high seas implies logically that only flag State has jurisdiction over ships flying its flag and that the warships and State owned ships operated by a State on non-commercial service have complete immunity from the jurisdiction of any other State (Articles 95-96). In the matter of collision between ships of different flag States, only the flag State or the State of which the officer responsible for the collision is national are to have jurisdiction. As slavery is banned, the 1982 Convention prohibits the transportation of slaves in ships and any slave taking refuge on board any ship becomes *ipso facto* free.[94] Piracy is a crime against human civilization and it is prohibited with the duty on all States to co-operate in its repression. Article 101 defines piracy. It consists of any of the following acts:

(a) any illegal acts of violence or detention, or any act of depredation, committed for private ends by the crew or the passengers of a private ship or a private aircraft and directed:

 (i) on the high seas, against another ship or aircraft, or against persons or property on board such ship or aircraft;

 (ii) against a ship, aircraft, persons or property in a place outside the jurisdiction of any State;

(b) any act of voluntary participation in the operation of a ship or of an aircraft with knowledge of facts making it a pirate ship or aircraft;

(c) any act of inciting or of intentionally facilitating an act described in subparagraph (i) or (ii).[95] A ship or an aircraft is considered a pirate ship or aircraft if it is intended by the persons in its dominant control to be used for the purpose of committing one of the acts referred to in article 101. The same applies if the ship or aircraft has been used to commit any such act, so long as it remains under the control of the persons guilty of that act.[96] Only warships or military aircrafts, or other ships or aircrafts clearly marked and identifiable as being on government service and authorized to that effect may carry out a seizure of pirate ship or aircraft on account of piracy. Traffic in narcotic drugs and psychotropic substances is prohibited. As such, all States are to cooperate in the suppression of illicit traffic in narcotic drugs and psychotropic substances engaged in by ships on the high seas contrary to international conventions. Also, any State which has reasonable grounds for believing that a ship flying its flag is engaged in illicit traffic in narcotic drugs or psychotropic substances may request the cooperation of other States to suppress such traffic.[97] Broadcasting from the high seas which is not authorized is prohibited; for the purposes of this Convention, "unauthorized broadcasting" means the transmission of sound radio or television broadcasts from a ship or an installation on the high seas intended for reception by the general public contrary to international regulations, but excluding the transmission of distress calls.[98]

28C. The duties for enforcement of prohibitions as above, are placed on the warships or any other duly authorized ships or aircrafts clearly marked and identifiable as being on government service of the States. For this warships, etc., of States are given the rights (a) of visit, search and (b) of hot pursuit. With regard to (a) a warship etc., in general is justified in sending proper investigating teams to board the offending ship when there is reasonable ground for suspecting that:

(a) the ship is engaged in piracy;
(b) the ship is engaged in the slave trade;
(c) the ship is engaged in unauthorized broadcasting and the flag State of the warship has jurisdiction under article 109;
(d) the ship is without nationality; or
(e) though flying a foreign flag or refusing to show its flag, the ship is, in reality, of the same nationality as the warship.

However, if the suspicions prove to be unfounded, and that the ship boarded is found not to have committed any unjustified act, it shall be compensated for any loss or damage that may have been sustained by such ship by the visit and search. These provisions apply *mutatis mutandis* to military aircraft as well.[99]

28D. The "hot pursuit of a foreign ship may be undertaken when the competent authorities of the coastal State have good reason to believe that the ship has violated the laws and regulations of that State. Such pursuit must be commenced when the foreign ship or one of its boats is within the internal waters, the archipelagic waters, the territorial sea or the contiguous zone of the pursuing State, and may only be continued outside the territorial sea or the contiguous zone if the pursuit has not been interrupted. It is not necessary that, at the time when the foreign ship within the territorial sea or the contiguous zone receives the order to stop, the ship giving the order should likewise be within the territorial sea or the contiguous zone. If the foreign ship is within a contiguous zone, as defined in article 33, the pursuit may only be undertaken if there has been a violation of the rights for the protection of which the zone was established." Further, the right of hot pursuit shall apply *mutatis mutandis* to violations in the exclusive economic zone or on the continental shelf, including safety zones around continental shelf installations, of the laws and regulations of the coastal State applicable in accordance with this Convention to the exclusive economic zone or the continental shelf, including such safety zones. The right of hot pursuit ceases as soon as the ship pursued enters the territorial sea of its own State or of a third State. As mentioned the right of only warships or military aircraft, or other ships or aircraft clearly marked and identifiable as being on government service and authorized to that effect may exercise hot pursuit. Where an aircraft affects hot pursuit: (a) the above provisions apply *mutatis mutandis*; (b) the aircraft giving the order to stop must itself actively pursue the ship until a ship or another aircraft of the coastal State, summoned by the aircraft, arrives to take over the pursuit, unless the aircraft is itself able to arrest the ship. It does not suffice to justify an arrest outside the territorial sea that the ship was merely sighted by the aircraft as an offender or suspected offender, if it was not both ordered to stop and pursued by the aircraft itself or other aircrafts or ships which continue the pursuit without interruption. The right to hot pursuit is subject to proper compensation to the pursued ship or aircraft when the hot pursuit is undertaken without proper justification.[100]

28E. Part VII dealing with the regime for High Seas also provides for conservation and management of the living resources of the high seas. All States have the right for their nationals to engage in fishing on the high seas but at the same time all States have the duty to take, or to cooperate with other States in taking, such measures for their respective nationals as may be necessary for the conservation of the living resources of the high seas. The appropriate measures for this purpose are indicated in Section 2 of this Part, particularly by Articles 118 and 119 and *inter alia*, in article 63, paragraph 2, and articles 64 to 67 of the 1982 Convention.

29. *Regime of Islands in High Seas*: An island is a naturally formed area of land, surrounded by water, which is above water at high tide. The islands are to have the territorial sea, the contiguous zone, the exclusive economic zone and the continental shelf as determined for continental territories provided these are not bare rocks but are capable of sustaining human habitation or economic life of their own.[101] The Indian island territories of Andaman & Nicobar and Lakshadweep are islands in high seas and have the continental shelf, etc., of their own.

30. *Enclosed or Semi-Enclosed Sea*: The 1982 Convention has recognized the potential conflicts that may ensue when two or more States make similar claims of territorial waters or EEZ in the enclosed or semi-enclosed sea accessible to them.[102] For the purposes of this Convention, "enclosed or semi-enclosed sea" means a gulf, basin or sea surrounded by two or more States and connected to another sea or the ocean by a narrow outlet or consisting entirely or primarily of the territorial seas and exclusive economic zones of two or more coastal States. The States should envisage or endeavour for coordinate management, conservation, exploration and exploitation of the living resources of the sea; and coordinate the implementation of their rights and duties with respect to the protection and preservation of the marine environment, directly or through an appropriate regional organization.

31. *Landlocked States under the 1982 Convention*: Since the ocean and sea are regarded as common heritage of mankind

and since the UNCLOS is UN sponsored attempt to codify the law of sea, naturally all member States of the UNO have a vested interest in whatever sea offers to mankind, the freedoms on sea or share in its wealth. Historically the problems of landlocked States have been twofold:

(1) The right to have ships with their flags and to use the port facilities of the coastal States but that requires bilateral agreements between the landlocked States and the coastal States. At one time Switzerland refused permission to its nationals to own and register the ships with other States on the ground that this would force Switzerland to depend upon the goodwill of maritime States. Oppenheim has observed that powers and obligations for the flag State with regard to the ship can be real only when the ship belongs to a port of a State where on return of the ship, the captains, crew and passengers could be punished for any offence on the sea.[103] However, after the First World War the matters took a turn. Various treaties recognized the lawful status of the ships on sea of those flying the flag of landlocked States.[104] Collectively, the Treaty of Versailles of 1919 by its Article 27 and the Barcelona Declaration of 20th April 1921, recognized the maritime flag of inland or landlocked States when the ships were registered at one specified place within the territories of inland States. Earlier, the 1958 Geneva Convention on the Law of Sea recognized this position. Now the 1982 Treaty on the Law of Sea, by Part X, entitled, 'Right of Access of Landlocked States to and from the Sea and Freedom of Transit'[105] proceeds on the basis of established right of landlocked States to register ships on their own territory. Such ships have freedom of navigation on high seas and have the right of innocent passage through straits, EEZ or territorial sea of other States. Such ships are entitled to enjoy equal treatment to that accorded to any other flag State in any maritime ports.[106]

(2) The landlocked States had so far found that for 'access' to the sea they had to depend on bilateral agreements with one or more intermediate and coastal States having seaports. Obviously, the granting or obtaining of such transit or use of seaports had depended on the goodwill of the transit giving States or coastal States. Historically, steps in the direction of

helping landlocked States in achieving transit and access to sea started with the Havana UN Conference on Trade and Employment of March 1948, by holding that the granting of special rights and facilities of transit to a State which has no direct access to the sea, will be lawful exception to the operation of most-favoured nations clause.[107] Although the UN General Assembly had endorsed the demands of landlocked States,[108] yet the 1958 UN Conference on Law of Sea could not solve the transit right of the landlocked States. Again in 1965, UN General Assembly affirmed the proposed Convention on Transit Trade of Landlocked States, prepared by the Fifth Committee of the UN Conference on Trade and Development of 1964. The General Assembly requested the UN Secretary General and the UNCTAD to implement the same in their practices. It can be noted that India and Nepal had signed a Treaty of Trade and Transit in 1971 and their follow on arrangements, giving wide transit facilities with freedoms of customs and other related aspects of the problem when the goods of Nepal passed through Indian seaports and airports.

31A. The situation has completely changed under the 1982 Convention on Law of Sea. Now its Part X covers all aspects of the problems of landlocked States in reaching out to sea. There has been a noticeable workable compromise between the interests of landlocked States and transit or coastal States.

(i) Right of access to and from the sea and freedom of transit along with the 'freedom of the high seas and the common heritage of mankind' are provided by Article 125:

(a) Landlocked States shall have the right of access to and from the sea for the purpose of exercising the rights provided for in this Convention including those relating to the freedom of the high seas and the common heritage of mankind. To this end, landlocked States shall enjoy freedom of transit through the territory of transit States by all means of transport.

(b) The terms and modalities for exercising freedom of transit shall be agreed between the landlocked States and transit States concerned through bilateral, sub regional or regional agreements.

(c) Transit States, in the exercise of their full sovereignty over their territory, shall have the right to take all measures necessary to ensure that the rights and facilities provided for in this Part for landlocked States shall in no way infringe their legitimate interests.

(ii) The exclusion of the application of most-favored nations clause for agreements between landlocked States and transit States is guaranteed by Article 126.

(iii) Articles 127 and 128 also confirm and confer important rights in favour of landlocked States.

(a) By former Article, the traffic in transit shall not be subject to any customs duties, taxes or other charges except charges levied for specific services rendered in connection with such traffic. Also, the means of transport in transit and other facilities provided for and used by landlocked States shall not be subject to taxes or charges higher than those levied for the use of means of transport of the transit State.

(b) Article 128 further grants that for the convenience of traffic of landlocked States while its goods are in transit or are in free zones, other customs facilities may be provided at the ports of entry and exit in the transit States, by agreement between those States and the landlocked States.

(iv) Constructive international co-operation on the part of transit and coastal States has also been made part of the obligation under the law of sea. On this score Article 129 provides that where there are no means of transport in transit States to give effect to the freedom of transit or where the existing means, including the port installations and equipment, are inadequate in any respect, the transit States and landlocked States concerned may cooperate in constructing or improving them.

Exploitation of High Seas

32. *General Observations*: Part XI of the 1982 Convention on the Law of the Sea is a novel addition to the law of sea based on the technological advancements enabling deep sea mining. This Part deals with mining of minerals lying on the deep ocean

floor outside of nationally regulated high sea or international seabed areas. It is vitally supplemented by the 1998 'Agreement relating to the Implementation of the Part XI of the Convention'[109] in order to accommodate the interests of industrialized States. There is a history behind this development which is the basis of the Part XI, and which is in short noted thus.

32A. With the development of technology for extracting minerals from the seabed, as distinguished from shallow waters beyond territorial sea margin, the high seas became *res nullius* instead of *res communis* that the industrialized States proceeded to exploit depending upon their seabed mining technology. The doctrine of continental shelf was an offshoot of this development. By mid-1960s the potential of extractable seabed wealth had become world-wide common knowledge. In the General Assembly on 1st November 1967, Malta's Ambassador to the United Nations, spoke about the superpowers rivalry that was spreading to the oceans, about the pollution that was poisoning the seas and about the conflicting legal claims on seabed with their adverse implications on a stable world order. He reminded the nations of the rich potential that lay on the seabed. He ended his speech with a call for "an effective international regime over the seabed and the ocean floor beyond a clearly defined national jurisdiction." "It is the only alternative by which we can hope to avoid the escalating tension that will be inevitable if the present situation is allowed to continue", he had said. The General Assembly took the matter seriously[110] and also adopted[111] a 'Declaration of Principles' referred to earlier. By this United Nations General Assembly declared the resources of the seabed beyond the limits of national jurisdiction to be "the common heritage of mankind", which could not be appropriated by any State. The next question was determination of the 'seabed beyond the limits of national jurisdiction' on which the answer came in the form of a compromise, that is the concept of Exclusive Economic Zone and that became Part V of the Treaty or Convention. In the EEZ minerals can be exploited and appropriated by the coastal States subject to payment of a share of profits to the International Seabed Authority. Further, the adoption of the Agreement on Part XI, Annexure 1 to the

Convention, has removed those obstacles, which had prevented the industrialized countries from adhering to the Convention. The High Sea became 'Area' dealt with finally under Part XI of the 1982 Convention in the interest for exploration and exploitation of the seas as the common heritage of mankind.

33. *The Part XI of 1982 Convention: Regime for the 'Area'*: The 'Area' as defined by Article 1 of the Convention to mean the seabed and ocean floor and subsoil thereof, beyond the limits of national jurisdiction; along with its resources it is declared to be the 'common heritage of mankind'. The legal status of 'Area' is defined by Article 137: (1) No State is to claim or exercise sovereignty or sovereign rights over any part of the Area or its resources, nor can any State or natural or juridical person appropriate any part thereof. No such claim or exercise of sovereignty or sovereign rights or such appropriation shall be recognized. (2) All rights in the resources of the Area are vested in mankind as a whole, on whose behalf the International Seabed Authority shall act. These resources are not subject to alienation. The minerals recovered from the Area, however, may only be alienated in accordance with this Part XI and the rules, regulations and procedures of the International Seabed Authority. In circumstances of non-compliance or breach of the prohibitions, the Authority is entitled to damages. It is specifically laid down that the functioning of the Authority be carried out for the benefit of mankind as a whole, irrespective of the geographical location of States, whether coastal or landlocked, and by taking into particular consideration the interests and needs of developing States and of peoples who have not attained full independence or other self-governing status recognized by the United Nations in accordance with General Assembly resolution 1514 (XV) and other relevant General Assembly resolutions. It is the duty of the Authority to provide for the equitable sharing of financial and other economic benefits derived from activities in the Area through an appropriate mechanism, on a non-discriminatory basis, in accordance with Article 160, paragraph 2(f)(i) of this Convention. Further, rights and legitimate interests of coastal States have to be taken care of by the Authority. Article 150 lays down the policies relating to

activities in the Area; and Article 151 provides for production policies for exploitation of the 'Area' in detail.

34. *The International Seabed Authority*: Article 156 of the Convention formally establishes the International Seabed Authority. The Authority is the organ through which States Parties to the Convention, in accordance with the regime for the seabed and ocean floor and subsoil thereof beyond the limits of national jurisdiction (the Area) established in Part XI and the annexed Agreement organize and control activities in the Area. This is to be done particularly with a view to administer the resources of the Area. Article 153 (2) provides that Activities in the Area shall be carried out (a) by the Enterprise, and (b) by States Parties in association with the Authority, or state enterprises or natural or juridical persons which possess the nationality of States Parties or are effectively controlled by them or their nationals, when sponsored by such States, or any group of the foregoing which meets the requirements provided in this Part XI and in Annex III. The 'Enterprise'[112] is an organ of the Authority, which is to conduct the operational business in the Area on behalf of the Authority under the direction and control of the Council, vide, Article 169.

34A. All States who sign the 1982 Convention are *ipso facto* its members. The International Seabed Authority has its headquarter in Jamaica. The Authority has three principal organs. First, an Assembly, made up of all members of the Authority, that is to say of all States which have acceded to the 1982 Convention, with power to set general policy. Second, a Council which is constituted of 36 members elected from among the members of the Authority. The Council has the power to take executive decisions, it is advised by an Economic Planning Commission and the Legal and Technical Commission and it administers, controls and conducts the work and the activities in the Area but in accordance with a formal written plan of work drawn up in accordance with Annex III which is part of the Convention. Third, the authority has a Secretariat that is headed by a Secretary-General.[113] The Authority has 'General Fund', 'Special Fund' and 'Borrowing Powers' for its finances.

Marine Environment, Scientific Research and Technology

35. The 1982 Convention has adopted a positive approach for protection of seas from pollution, advancement of human knowledge about the added value of sea for betterment of human life through marine research and for making all coastal States and users of the sea to acquire international standards for keeping appropriate marine environment by easily acquiring of marine technology for that purpose. In the 'Area' it is the duty of the Authority to ensure effective protection for the marine environment from harmful effects which may arise from its activities. It has to take measures for the prevention, reduction and control of pollution and other hazards to the marine environment, including the coastline; it has also to carry out its activities in the Area with reasonable regard for the marine environment and the protection of human life. It is required to synchronize its programmes with the ecological balance of the marine environment. The Authority may carry out marine scientific research concerning the Area and its resources, and may enter into contracts for that purpose but marine scientific research in the Area shall be carried out exclusively for peaceful purposes and for the benefit of mankind as a whole, in accordance with Part XIII of the 1982 Convention. It shall also transfer appropriate technology to developing States as might be sought and be necessary for protection of marine environment.[114]

35A. The Part XII of the 1982 Convention is devoted to the control of pollution, protection and preservation of marine environment. States have the obligation to protect and preserve the marine environment, and for that the States shall take, individually or jointly as appropriate, all measures consistent with this Convention that are necessary to prevent, reduce and control pollution of the marine environment from any source, using for this purpose the best practicable means at their disposal and in accordance with their capabilities, and they shall endeavour to harmonize their policies in this connection. Further, the States have to prevent pollution from installations and devices used in exploration or exploitation of the natural resources of the seabed and subsoil, pollution arising from incidents or activities under their jurisdiction or control or the pollution from vessels.[115] Part XIII provides for right of all States to engage in marine scientific research for peaceful purposes; obviously, this is different from the use of sea for testing nuclear explosive devices, etc. Further, Part XIV lays the foundation for 'Development and Transfer of Marine Technology', through international organization and co-operation among States with the view to accelerate the social and economic development of underdeveloped States. For the achievement of the purposes of this Part, it also provides for the establishment of the regional centres to function in co-ordination with competent international organizations, the Authority and other institutions.

Settlement of Disputes

36. A viable regime has not only the subjects of the system and the set of obligatory rules but also a system for doing justice by interpretation of rules and their application to the disputes, which the parties on their part accept as decisive. The 1982 Convention is sanctioned by the United Nations to which the States have acceded by their constitutional procedures. As such the settlement of disputes arising out of the 1982 Convention has to be done within the framework of Article 33 of Chapter VI of the Charter of United Nations. The Charter of the United Nations requires that all Members of the Organization are to settle their international disputes by peaceful methods in such a manner that international peace and security are not endangered. Accordingly, Part XV of the 1982 Convention on the Law of the Sea requires that State Parties to it are to settle any dispute between them concerning the interpretation or application of the Convention by peaceful methods in accordance with Article 2 (3) of the Charter of the United Nations and shall normally find a solution to the dispute by the means indicated in Article 33 (1) of the Charter. Under the Articles 280 and 283 of 1982 Convention when the Parties fail to settle their disputes by the methods of their choice only then its Part XV comes into play.

36A. It is essential that where possible the Parties should first exhaust 'local remedies' as required in general international law. The Parties can thereafter submit the dispute to non-binding procedures of Articles 279-285 and Annexure V of the 1982 Convention. The matters of dispute include disputes between States Parties concerning (i) the interpretation or application of the provisions of the Convention, along with those of the Agreement relating to the Implementation of the Part XI of the Convention,[116] (ii) the deep seabed Area; or (iii) the other categories of disputes as mentioned in article 187, Section 5, Part XI of 1982 Convention. For this the Parties may seek one of the methods prescribed in Article 287. It is also possible for the Parties under Article 287 of the Convention to make advance declarations for accepting the jurisdiction of:

(a) The International Tribunal for the Law of the Sea (established in accordance with Annex VI of the Convention) including the Seabed Disputes Chamber;

(b) The International Court of Justice;

(c) An arbitral tribunal constituted in accordance with Annex VII of the Convention;

(d) A special arbitral tribunal constituted in accordance with Annex VIII for one or more of the categories of disputes specified therein.

37. *International Tribunal for the Law of the Sea:* The International Tribunal for the Law of the Sea[117] is a new forum for adjudication of disputes under the 1982 Convention. Its seat is at Hamburg, Germany. The Tribunal may sit and exercise its functions elsewhere as well whenever it considers this desirable. The jurisdiction of the Tribunal extends to all disputes and all applications submitted to it in accordance with the 1982 United Nations Convention on the Law of the Sea and all matters specifically provided for in any other agreements which may confer jurisdiction on the Tribunal. The Tribunal will apply the provisions of the 1982 Convention on the Law of the Sea and other rules of international law not incompatible with the Convention in deciding disputes submitted to it. It also has the power to decide a case *ex aequo et bono*, if the parties so agree.

37A. The Tribunal has exclusive jurisdiction, through its Seabed Disputes Chamber, on all disputes relating to activities in the international seabed Area. Also, the Tribunal, through its

Seabed Disputes Chamber, has jurisdiction to render 'advisory opinion' at the request of the Assembly or the Council of the International Seabed Authority on legal questions arising within the scope of their respective activities. The Tribunal has special jurisdiction in matters calling for provisional measures, for example, where the authorities of a State Party have detained a vessel flying the flag of another State Party and it is alleged that the detaining State has not complied with the provisions of the Convention for the prompt release of the vessel or its crew upon the posting of a reasonable bond or other financial security, etc. The decisions of the Tribunal are final and are to be complied with by all the parties to the dispute. However, decisions of the Tribunal do not have a binding force except between the parties in respect of the particular dispute. Unless otherwise decided by the Tribunal, each party has to bear its own costs.

International Organizations and the Final Act

38. Parts XVI and XVII give sanctity to the obligations under the 1982 Convention. According to Part XVI, the States and the International Organizations[118] which accede to the Convention are (i) to evince good faith in executing its provisions, (ii) to make use of the sea for peaceful uses and in accordance with international law and (iii) are to be willing to take up responsibilities and liabilities to pay damages where required. The accession mode to the Convention and its coming into force is regulated by Part XVII.

Follow-up Participation by India on 1982 Convention

39. India has been a signatory of the four 1958 Geneva Conventions on the Law of Sea and had fully participated in the UNCLOS conferences and meetings. It has duly acceded to the 1982 Convention on the Law of Sea. India had accepted the customary law of the sea, as it existed before 1958. It had three nautical miles territorial waters limit till 1956 when it was extended to six nautical miles and further to 12 nautical miles in 1976. Following the trend set by the US claim of continental shelf and contiguous zones, in 1955, President of India had made proclamation claiming continental shelf for India. The Proclamations by the President of India are made under

Article 297 of the Constitution as amended from time to time that is, in 1963 and 1976, to lay claims under new emerging developments. Under the 1958 Convention on Continental Shelf, there was no need to make any proclamation and the provisions of the 1958 Convention applied. Similar was the position with reference to the Contiguous Zones of India under Article 24 of the 1958 Geneva Territorial Sea Convention, for the preservation of fisheries, etc. It may be mentioned that India has more than 4000 miles of coastline and it has about 1280 islands, which include the Andaman & Nicobar and Lakshadweep. The Bay of Bengal is shallow sea and the Arabian Sea is also not very deep and has a very low gradient. Fish from oceans also come to its river basins for breeding in large numbers. Diving into sea for pearls has been an industry from ancient times in India.

40. The UNCLOS III had given new impetus to all coastal States of the world. India had adopted the Territorial Waters, Continental Shelf, Exclusive Economic Zone and other Maritime Zones Act, 1976, now popularly referred to as Maritime Zones Act, 1976, and had claimed all the jurisdictions which had emerged in the ICNT of the UNCLOS III in 1976. India has depended on the 1982 Convention for its rights and duties in the maritime zones identified under the Act. While India had sovereign rights over the territorial waters it has had only those rights as were or are available through the 1958 Geneva Conventions or now under 1982 Convention, in other maritime zones. Accordingly, the Maritime Zones Act defines the different zones on sea appurtenant to India now, and the scope and manner of exercising powers therein. As India has acceded to the 1982 Convention, accordingly it is a member of the International Seabed Authority, which under Part XI of the Convention regulates the exploration and exploitation of high seas. India is also bound by the rules and regulations set by the International Maritime Organization (IMO), which is a Specialized Agency of the UNO for universal traffic or navigation rules on sea irrespective of maritime zones.

41. The Maritime Zones Act, 1976, by Sections 3 and 4 defines the limits along with the nature of sovereign rights on territorial waters; by Section 5 it defines the contiguous zone

for India and the extent of jurisdiction in the matters related to (a) security of India and (b) the immigration, sanitation, customs and other fiscal aspects. In both zones the Central Government can by notification make changes for new developments. Section 6 describes all sovereign, exclusive and qualified rights and jurisdiction of India in the Indian continental shelf area. Its clause (5) provides that the Central Government can by notification in the Official Gazette (a) designate its continental shelf and (b) make such provisions as deemed necessary for (i) the exploration, exploitation and protection of the resources of the continental shelf area, or (ii) the safety protection of artificial islands, off-shore terminals, installations and other structures and devices in such designated area, or (iii) the protection of marine environment from pollution in the designated area, or (iv) the customs and other fiscal matters in relation to such designated area. Section 7 of the Act defines and appropriates an Exclusive Economic Zone for India in terms and conditions of the 1982 Convention. Clause (4) defines the 'exclusive' nature of the rights and powers to be exercised by the Central Government by notification in the Official Gazette. The Union Government has sovereign rights for the purposes of exploration, exploitation, conservation and management of living and non-living natural resources as well as producing energy from tides, winds and currents in the EEZ. The Union Government has exclusive rights in the EEZ for (i) construction, maintenance, or operation of artificial islands, off-shore terminals, installations and other structures and devices, (ii) authorizing, regulating and controlling scientific research in the Exclusive Economic Zone of India, (iii) preserving and protecting the marine environment from pollution in the designated area, (iv) exercising such rights in Exclusive Economic Zone of India as are recognized by International Law and (v) regulating customs and other fiscal matters in the Exclusive Economic Zone of India. Section 15 grants to the Central Government wide powers to frame rules for carrying out all or any of the purposes of the Act by notification in the Official Gazette and these shall be binding on all persons, Indians or foreigners, who may be present in the Indian marine zones.

NOTES

1. Ancient Indian mythology has vivid accounts of the earth totally covered by sea with only a few mountains seen above its surface, before 'moon' was 'churned out' of the sea. Subsequent to this activity, continents had surfaced out of the sea. It notes how Indian civilization was intimately linked to the space, ocean and earth, which were considered to be common heritage of mankind. A UN document on Law of Sea notes: "The ocean, with its enormity and mystery, has ever been part of human consciousness".
2. A UN Document entitled, 'Law of Sea: A Historical Perspective' notes: "Conflicting claims, even extravagant ones, over the oceans were not new. In 1494, two years after Christopher Columbus' first expedition to America, Pope Alexander VI met with representatives of two of the great maritime Powers of the day — Spain and Portugal — and neatly divided the Atlantic Ocean between them. A Papal Bull gave Spain everything west of the line the Pope drew down the Atlantic and Portugal everything east of it. On that basis, the Pacific and the Gulf of Mexico were acknowledged as Spain's, while Portugal was given the South Atlantic and the Indian Ocean: *UN Org./LOS/Convention;* see Appendices 9-587, also.
3. 75 *UNTS*, 85.
4. Chapter II, IInd Geneva Convention, 1949.
5. Chapter III, Articles 22-27: IInd Geneva Convention, 1949.
6. Chapter V, IInd Geneva Convention, 1949.
7. Article 18, IInd Geneva Convention, 1949.
8. Article 9 'Activities of the International Committee of Red Cross'. IInd Geneva Convention, 1949.
9. This Convention has been further supplemented by Protocol I relating to the Protection of International Armed Conflicts, and it extends to all wounded, sick and shipwrecked persons.
10. Article 47, IInd Geneva Convention, 1949.
11. GAOR Resolution: 2340 (XXII), 18th December 1967 was followed by the 'Treaty on the Prohibition of the Emplacement of Nuclear Weapons on the Sea-bed and Ocean Floor and Sub-soil Thereof', it prohibited actions and uses of sea floor detrimental to common interests of mankind.
12. GAOR Resolutions: 2832 (XXVI), 16th December 1971; 3259 (XXIX), 9th December 1974; and of 12th December 1977.
13. Soviet Russia has disintegrated in early 1990s and it ceased to be an enemy of the West.
14. Text of the two Proclamations: *American Journal of International Law*, Vol. 40 (1946), pp. 45-46.
15. Presidential Proclamation of 30th August 1955.

16. U.N. Gupta, Chapter: 'The Changing Law of the Sea': *Developments on the Frontiers of International Law*, p. 148.
17. Reiff, *United States and the Treaty Law of the Sea*, pp. 4-5.
18. See, Garcia Amador, *The Exploration and Conservation of Resources of Sea*, p. 153.
19. The limits varied from 3 miles to 200 miles.
20. GAOR Resolution: 1105 (XI).
21. Conference was held from 24th February to 29th April 1958.
22. 450 *UNTS*, 11. It became operative with effect from 20th March 1962 after receiving necessary number of ratifications.
23. 516 *UNTS*, 311. It became operative with effect from 10th September 1964 after receiving necessary number of ratifications.
24. 599 *UNTS*. It became operative with effect from 20th March 1964 after receiving necessary number of ratifications.
25. 499 *UNTS*, 311. It became operative with effect from 10th June 1964 after receiving necessary number of ratifications.
26. The text of Convention is in 52nd *American Journal of International Law*, 842.
27. It is now covered by another Convention.
28. Article 9 of the Convention.
29. IMCO is a Specialized Agency of the United Nations. Now it is named International Maritime Organization (IMO).
30. (1927) Series A, No. 10.
31. Articles 15 to 22.
32. Articles 24-26.
33. Some of the Conventions related to prevention and control of pollution are: The Convention for the Prevention of Pollution from Ships, (1973) (MARPOL) and 1978 Protocol attached to it; International Convention Relating to Intervention on the High Seas in cases of Oil Pollution Casualties; or, Oslo Convention for the Prevention of Marine Pollution by Dumping from Ships and Aircraft, 1972.
34. Fenwick, *International Law*, 2 ed., pp. 421-422; Max Sorensen, *Manual of Public International Law*, 1968, pp. 349-350; 75 British and Foreign State Papers, 556.
35. Fenwick, *International Law*, 3 ed., pp. 377-378; U.N. Gupta, *op.cit.*, f.n. 16, at p. 154.
36. *UK* v. *Iceland*, 1974 ICJ Reports 3; and *Federal Republic of Germany* v. *Iceland*, 1974 ICJ Reports 175.
37. *Anglo-Norwegian Fisheries Case*, 1951 ICJ Reports 116.
38. Articles 4-6 of the Convention; the principle was already approved by the ICJ in the *Anglo-Norwegian Fisheries Case, op.cit.*
39. Article 24 of the Convention.

40. Articles 1-14 of the Convention on Fishing and Conservation of the Living Resources of the High Seas.
41. Article 2 of the Convention.
42. That is, updating or bringing up the Conventions to meet growing or contemporaneous needs.
43. *North Sea Continental Shelf Cases* (1969) ICJ Reports, 3.
44. W. Friedman, *The Future of Oceans*, 1971, pp. 1-9.
45. Presence of tremendous wealth in oceans is confirmed by Indian mythology. According to it originally there were mountains protruding out of boundless sea on the earth globe. Then there was extensive churning of the sea by good and bad celestial beings (forces). First poisonous substances (volcano fumes and matter) came out. After that, 'moon' came out of the sea. As water filled into the space left by moon, the land mass came out along with the Goddess of wealth, Lakshmi, who later and now resides on a sea-platform made by snake-god, the normal watchman of wealth. Goddess Lakshmi rules the development, maintenance, distribution and confiscation of wealth. By the present calculations and assessments, geologically land and seabed have continuity and sea contains millions times more wealth than dry earth. Petrol, nickel, diamonds and tin are some of such wealth having continuity on seabed and earth floors. Anthropologically, under Indian mythology man was amphibious; he could with ease live and walk both on seabed and dry land and so both under sea and land based wealth was within his reach.
46. GA Resolution: 2467 (XXIII), 'Committee on the Peaceful Uses of Seabed and the Ocean-floor beyond the Limits of National Jurisdiction'.
47. GA Resolution: 2574-A (XXIV), 15th December 1969.
48. GA Resolution: 2574-C (XXIV), 15th December 1969.
49. GA Resolution: 2574-D (XXIV), 15th December 1969.
50. GA Resolution: 2749 (XXV), 17th December 1970.
51. GA Resolution: 2950-C (XXV).
52. Sub-Committee I Report on the proposals of Malta: GAOR XXV Supplement No. 21 and 22; Sub-Committee II Report on proposals on fishing problems and for limits of contiguous zones: UN Doc. No. A/Conf. 19/8 p. 157; Sorenson, *Law of the Sea*, p. 244.
53. GA Resolution: 2467 (XXIII).
54. GA Resolution: 2750 (XXV) of 17th December 1970: Problems of landlocked States.
55. UN Doc. A/AC 138/37, p. 9.
56. UN Doc. A/Conf. 62/18 1974 (XXIX).
57. GA Resolution: 2249 (XXV), December 17th, 1970.
58. Resolution I has established a Preparatory Commission for the Seabed

Authority and the Law of Sea Tribunal with its seat at Hamburg; Resolution II regulates the preparatory investment in the pioneering activities of the States and private consortium relating to seabed minerals, primarily polymetallic nodules; Resolution III defines the rights and interests of non-self-governing territories in the sea; and, Resolution IV permits the right to sign the Final Act of the Treaty by recognized national liberation movements as observers.

59. Particularly Articles 5 to 7: 1982 Convention.
60. Article 10: 1982 Convention.
61. Anglo-Norwegian Fisheries Case: (1951) ICJ Reports, 116. The principle recognized by the ICJ is taken as international law under Article 2(3) of the 1982 Convention.
62. Article 2: 1982 Convention.
63. Article 17: 1982 Convention.
64. Article 18: 1982 Convention.
65. Article 19: 1982 Convention.
66. Article 21: 1982 Convention.
67. Article 20: 1982 Convention.
68. Article 23: 1982 Convention.
69. Articles 27-32: 1982 Convention.
70. Articles 24 and 25: 1982 Convention.
71. Article 37: 1982 Convention.
72. About 40% of the oil traffic of the world takes place through this strait.
73. Article 34: 1982 Convention.
74. Article 35: 1982 Convention.
75. Article 36: 1982 Convention.
76. Article 38: 1982 Convention.
77. Articles 39 to 45: 1982 Convention.
78. Articles 46-56: 1982 Convention.
79. Article 46 defines "archipelago" as a group of islands, including parts of islands, interconnecting waters and other natural features which are so closely interrelated that such islands, waters and other natural features form an intrinsic geographical, economic and political entity, or which historically have been regarded as such.
80. Indonesia has about 13,000 islands.
81. Article 49: 1982 Convention.
82. Article 52: 1982 Convention.
83. Articles 55-75: 1982 Convention.
84. *The Fisheries Jurisdiction Cases*, (1974) ICJ, p. 3.
85. Article 71: 1982 Convention.

86. Articles 69 and 70: 1982 Convention.
87. Article 82: 1982 Convention.
88. Article 77: 1982 Convention.
89. *North Sea Continental Shelf Cases,* (1969) ICJ Reports, 3 at pp. 47-53: The Court stated:

    In the course of the negotiations (for equitable solution) the factors to be taken into account include:

    (1) the general configuration of the coasts of the Parties, as well as the presence of any special or unusual features;
    (2) so far as known or readily ascertainable, the physical and geographical structure, and natural resources, of the continental shelf areas involved;
    (3) the element of a reasonable degree of proportionality, which a delimitation carried out in accordance with equitable principle ought to bring about between the extent of the continental shelf areas appertaining to the coastal State and the length of its coast measured in the general direction of the coastline, account being taken for this purpose of the effects, actual or prospective, of any other continental shelf delimitation between adjacent States in the same region.
90. *The Continental Shelf (Libya* v. *Malta) Case,* 1985 ICJ Reports, 13 at p. 67.
91. Article 79: 1982 Convention.
92. Article 87: 1982 Convention.
93. Article 94: 1982 Convention.
94. Article 99: 1982 Convention.
95. Article 101: 1982 Convention.
96. Article 103: 1982 Convention.
97. Article 108: 1982 Convention.
98. Article 109: 1982 Convention.
99. Article 110: 1982 Convention.
100. Article 111: 1982 Convention.
101. Part VIII, Article 121: 1982 Convention.
102. Part IX, Articles 121 and 122: 1982 Convention.
103. *International Law,* Vol. 1, Ed. viii, p. 592; also, Westlake, *International Law,* Vol. 1, p. 160.
104. Colombos, *International Law of Sea,* Ed. iv, pp. 293-294.
105. Articles 124 to 132: 1982 Convention.
106. Article 131: 1982 Convention.
107. UN Doc. A/Conf. 13/29; and also E/C No. 11/425, para 103.
108. Resolutions: 1028 (XI) and 1105 (XI) of 20th and 21st February 1957.
109. It is Annexure I to the 1982 Convention.

110. Resolutions: 2467 (XXIII), December 1968; 2574 (XXIV) and 2574D (XXIV) December 1969.
111. Resolution: 2249 (XXV) December 17th 1970.
112. Statute of 'Enterprise': Annexure IV if the 1982 Convention.
113. Articles 156 to 160: 1982 Convention.
114. Articles 143-147: 1982 Convention.
115. Articles 192 to 194: 1982 Convention.
116. Annexure I of 1982 Convention.
117. Annexure VI to the 1982 Convention establishes the Tribunal.
118. Annexure IX to 1982 Convention defines the conditions for 'Participation by International Organizations' in the Convention.

LAW OF SEA CONVENTION, 1982

PART-I

INTRODUCTION

ARTICLE 1

Use of terms and scope

1. For the purposes of this Convention:

   (1) "Area" means the seabed and ocean-floor, and subsoil thereof, beyond the limits of national jurisdiction;

   (2) "Authority" means the International Seabed Authority;

   (3) "activities in the Area" means all activities of exploration for, and exploitation of, the resources of the Area;

   (4) "pollution of the marine environment" means the introduction by man, directly or indirectly, of substances or energy into the marine environment, including estuaries, which results or is likely to result in such deleterious effects as—harm to living resources and marine life, hazards to human health, hindrance to marine activities, including fishing and other legitimate uses of the sea, impairment of quality for use of sea water and reduction of amenities;

   (5) (a) "dumping" means:

      (i) any deliberate disposal of wastes or other matter from vessels, aircraft, platforms or other man-made structures at sea, and

      (ii) any deliberate disposal of vessels, aircraft, platforms or other man-made structures at sea;

   (b) "dumping" does not include:

      (i) the disposal of wastes or other matter

incidental to, or derived from the normal operations of vessels, aircraft, platforms or other man-made structures at sea and their equipment, other than wastes or other matter transported by or to vessels, aircraft, platforms or other man-made structures at sea, operating for the purpose of disposal of such matter or derived from the treatment of such wastes or other matter on such vessels, aircraft, platforms or structures, and

(ii) placement of matter for a purpose other than the mere disposal thereof, provided that such placement is not contrary to the aims of this Convention.

2. (1) "States Parties" means States which have consented to be bound by this Convention and for which this Convention is in force.

(2) This Convention applies *mutatis mutandis* to the entities referred to in article 305, paragraph l(b), (c), (d), (e) and (f), which become Parties to this Convention in accordance with the conditions relevant to each, and to that extent "States Parties" refers to those entities.

LAW OF SEA CONVENTION, 1982

PART-II

Territorial Sea and Contiguous Zone

SECTION 1. GENERAL PROVISIONS

ARTICLE 2

Legal status of the territorial sea, of the air space over the territorial sea and of its bed and subsoil

1. The sovereignty of a coastal State extends, beyond its land territory and internal waters and, in the case of an archipelagic State, its archipelagic waters, to an adjacent belt of sea, described as the territorial sea.
2. This sovereignty extends to the air space over the territorial sea as well as to its bed and subsoil.
3. The sovereignty over the territorial sea is exercised subject to this Convention and to other rules of international law.

SECTION 2. LIMITS OF THE TERRITORIAL SEA

ARTICLE 3

Breadth of the territorial sea

Every State has the right to establish the breadth of its territorial sea up to a limit not exceeding 12 nautical miles, measured from baselines determined in accordance with this Convention.

ARTICLE 4

Outer limit of the territorial sea

The outer limit of the territorial sea is the line, every point of which is at a distance from the nearest point of the baseline equal to the breadth of the territorial sea.

ARTICLE 5

Normal baseline

Except where otherwise provided in this Convention, the

normal baseline for measuring the breadth of the territorial sea is the low-water line along the coast as marked on large-scale charts officially recognized by the coastal State.

ARTICLE 6

Reefs

In the case of islands situated on atolls or of islands having fringing reefs, the baseline for measuring the breadth of the territorial sea is the seaward low-water line of the reef, as shown by the appropriate symbol on charts officially recognized by the coastal State.

ARTICLE 7

Straight baselines

1. In localities where the coastline is deeply indented and cut into, or if there is a fringe of islands along the coast in its immediate vicinity, the method of straight baselines joining appropriate points may be employed in drawing the baseline from which the breadth of the territorial sea is measured.
2. Where because of the presence of a delta and other natural conditions the coastline is highly unstable, the appropriate points may be selected along the furthest seaward extent of the low-water line and, notwithstanding subsequent regression of the low-water line, the straight baselines shall remain effective until changed by the coastal State in accordance with this Convention.
3. The drawing of straight baselines must not depart to any appreciable extent from the general direction of the coast, and the sea areas lying within the lines must be sufficiently closely linked to the land domain to be subject to the regime of internal waters.
4. Straight baselines shall not be drawn to and from low-tide elevations, unless lighthouses or similar installations which are permanently above sea level have been built on them or except in instances where the drawing of baselines to and from such elevations has received general international recognition.

5. Where the method of straight baselines is applicable under paragraph 1, account may be taken, in determining particular baselines, of economic interests peculiar to the region concerned, the reality and the importance of which are clearly evidenced by long usage.
6. The system of straight baselines may not be applied by a State in such a manner as to cut off the territorial sea of another State from the high seas or an exclusive economic zone.

ARTICLE 8

Internal waters

1. Except as provided in Part IV, waters on the landward side of the baseline of the territorial sea form part of the internal waters of the State.
2. Where the establishment of a straight baseline in accordance with the method set forth in article 7 has the effect of enclosing as internal waters areas which had not, previously, been considered as such, a right of innocent passage as provided in this Convention shall exist in those waters.

ARTICLE 9

Mouths of rivers

If a river flows directly into the sea, the baseline shall be a straight-line across the mouth of the river between points on the low-water line of its banks.

ARTICLE 10

Bays

1. This article relates only to bays, the coasts of which belong to a single State.
2. For the purposes of this Convention, a bay is a well-marked indentation whose penetration is in such proportion to the width of its mouth as to contain landlocked waters and constitute more than a mere curvature of the coast. An indentation shall not, however, be regarded as a bay unless its area is as large as, or larger than, that of the semi-circle whose diameter is a line drawn across the mouth of that indentation.

3. For the purpose of measurement, the area of an indentation is that lying between the low-water mark around the shore of the indentation and a line joining the low-water mark of its natural entrance points. Where, because of the presence of islands, an indentation has more than one mouth, the semi-circle shall be drawn on a line as long as the sum total of the lengths of the lines across the different mouths. Islands within an indentation shall be included as if they were part of the water area of the indentation.
4. If the distance between the low-water marks of the natural entrance points of a bay does not exceed 24 nautical miles, a closing line may be drawn between these two low-water marks, and the waters enclosed thereby shall be considered as internal waters.
5. Where the distance between the low-water marks of the natural entrance points of a bay exceeds 24 nautical miles, a straight baseline of 24 nautical miles shall be drawn within the bay in such a manner as to enclose the maximum area of water that is possible with a line of that length.
6. The foregoing provisions do not apply to the so-called "historic" bays, or, in any case, where the system of straight baselines provided for in article 7 is applied.

ARTICLE 11

Ports

For the purpose of delimiting the territorial sea, the outermost permanent harbour works which form an integral part of the harbour system are regarded as forming part of the coast. Off-shore installations and artificial islands shall not be considered as permanent harbour works.

ARTICLE 12

Roadsteads

Roadsteads which are normally used for the loading, unloading and anchoring of ships, and which would otherwise be situated wholly or partly outside the outer limit of the territorial sea, are included in the territorial sea.

ARTICLE 13

Low-tide elevations

1. A low-tide elevation is a naturally formed area of land which is surrounded by and above water at low tide but submerged at high tide. Where a low-tide elevation is situated wholly or partly at a distance not exceeding the breadth of the territorial sea from the mainland or an island, the low-water line on that elevation may be used as the baseline for measuring the breadth of the territorial sea.
2. Where a low-tide elevation is wholly situated at a distance exceeding the breadth of the territorial sea from the mainland or an island, it has no territorial sea of its own.

ARTICLE 14

Combination of methods for determining baselines

The coastal State may determine baselines in turn by any of the methods provided for in the foregoing articles to suit different conditions.

ARTICLE 15

Delimitation of the territorial sea between States with opposite or adjacent coasts

Where the coasts of two States are opposite or adjacent to each other, neither of the two States is entitled, failing agreement between them to the contrary, to extend its territorial sea beyond the median line every point of which is equidistant from the nearest points on the baselines from which the breadth of the territorial seas of each of the two States is measured. The above provision does not apply, however, where it is necessary by reason of historic title or other special circumstances to delimit the territorial seas of the two States in a way which is at variance therewith.

ARTICLE 16

Charts and lists of geographical coordinates

1. The baselines for measuring the breadth of the territorial sea determined in accordance with articles 7, 9 and 10,

or the limits derived therefrom, and the lines of delimitation drawn in accordance with articles 12 and 15 shall be shown on charts of a scale or scales adequate for ascertaining their position. Alternatively, a list of geographical coordinates of points, specifying the geodetic datum, may be substituted.

2. The coastal State shall give due publicity to such charts or lists of geographical coordinates and shall deposit a copy of each such chart or list with the Secretary-General of the United Nations.

SECTION 3. INNOCENT PASSAGE IN THE TERRITORIAL SEA

Sub-Section A. *Rules Applicable to All Ships*

ARTICLE 17

Right of innocent passage

Subject to this Convention, ships of all States, whether coastal or landlocked, enjoy the right of innocent passage through the territorial sea.

ARTICLE 18

Meaning of passage

1. Passage means navigation through the territorial sea for the purpose of—
   (a) traversing that sea without entering internal waters or calling at a roadstead or a port facility outside internal waters; or
   (b) proceeding to or from internal waters or a call at such roadstead or port facility.
2. Passage shall be continuous and expeditious. However, passage includes stopping and anchoring, but only in so far as the same are incidental to ordinary navigation or are rendered necessary by force *majeure* or distress, or for the purpose of rendering assistance to persons, ships, or aircraft in danger or distress.

ARTICLE 19

Meaning of innocent passage

1. Passage is innocent so long as it is not prejudicial to the peace, good order, or security of the coastal State.

Such passage shall take place in conformity with this Convention and with other rules of international law.

2. Passage of a foreign ship shall be considered to be prejudicial to the peace, good order, or security of the coastal State if in the territorial sea, it engages in any of the following activities:
   (a) any threat or use of force against the sovereignty, territorial integrity or political independence of the coastal State, or in any other manner in violation of the principles of international law embodied in the Charter of the United Nations;
   (b) any exercise or practice with weapons of any kind;
   (c) any act aimed at collecting information to the prejudice of the defence or security of the coastal State;
   (d) any act of propaganda aimed at affecting the defence or security of the coastal State;
   (e) the launching, landing, or taking on board of any aircraft;
   (f) the launching, landing, or taking on board of any military device;
   (g) the loading or unloading of any commodity, currency, or person contrary to the customs, fiscal, immigration, or sanitary laws and regulations of the coastal State;
   (h) any act of wilful and serious pollution contrary to this Convention;
   (i) any fishing activities;
   (j) the carrying out research or survey activities;
   (k) any act aimed at interfering with any systems of communication or any other facilities or installations of the coastal State; or
   (l) any other activity not having a direct bearing on passage.

ARTICLE 20

Submarines and other underwater vehicles

In the territorial sea, submarines and other underwater

vehicles are required to navigate on the surface and to show their flag.

ARTICLE 21

Laws and regulations of the coastal State relating to innocent passage

1. The coastal State may adopt laws and regulations, in conformity with the provisions of this Convention and other rules of international law, relating to innocent passage through the territorial sea, in respect of all or any of the following:
   (a) the safety of navigation and the regulation of maritime traffic;
   (b) the protection of navigational aids and facilities, and other facilities or installations;
   (c) the protection of cables and pipelines;
   (d) the conservation of the living resources of the sea;
   (e) the prevention of infringement of the fisheries laws and regulations of the coastal State;
   (f) the preservation of the environment of the coastal State and the prevention, reduction, and control of pollution thereof;
   (g) the marine scientific research and hydrographic surveys; or
   (h) the prevention of infringement of the customs, fiscal, immigration, or sanitary laws and regulations of the coastal State.
2. Such laws and regulations shall not apply to the design, construction, manning or equipment of foreign ships unless they are giving effect to generally accepted international rules or standards.
3. The coastal State shall give due publicity to all such laws and regulations.
4. Foreign ships exercising the right of innocent passage through the territorial sea shall comply with all such laws and regulations, and all generally accepted international regulations relating to the prevention of collisions at sea.

ARTICLE 22

Sea lanes and traffic separation schemes in the territorial sea

1. The coastal State may, where necessary having regard to the safety of navigation, require foreign ships exercising the right of innocent passage through its territorial sea to use such sea lanes and traffic separation schemes as it may designate or prescribe for the regulation of the passage of ships.
2. In particular, tankers, nuclear-powered ships and ships carrying nuclear or other inherently dangerous or noxious, substances or materials may be required to confine their passage to such sea lanes.
3. In the designation of sea lanes and the prescription of traffic separation schemes under this article, the coastal State shall take into account:
   (a) the recommendations of the competent international organization;
   (b) the channels customarily used for international navigation;
   (c) the special characteristics of particular ships and channels; and
   (d) the density of traffic.
4. The coastal State shall clearly indicate such sea lanes and traffic separation schemes on charts to which due publicity shall be given.

ARTICLE 23

Foreign nuclear-powered ships and ships carrying nuclear or other inherently dangerous or noxious substances

Foreign nuclear-powered ships and ships carrying nuclear or other inherently dangerous or noxious substances shall, when exercising the right of innocent passage through the territorial sea, carry documents and observe special precautionary measures established for such ships by international agreements.

ARTICLE 24

Duties of the coastal state

1. The coastal State shall not hamper the innocent passage

of foreign ships through the territorial sea except in accordance with this Convention. In particular, in the application of this Convention or of any laws or regulations adopted in conformity with this Convention, the coastal State shall not:

(a) impose requirements on foreign ships which have the practical effect of denying or impairing the right of innocent passage; or

(b) discriminate in form or in fact against the ships of any State or against ships carrying cargoes to, from or on behalf of any State.

2. The coastal State shall give appropriate publicity to any danger to navigation, of which it has knowledge, within its territorial sea.

ARTICLE 25

Rights of protection of the coastal state

1. The coastal State may take the necessary steps in its territorial sea to prevent passage which is not innocent.
2. In the case of ships proceeding to internal waters or a call at a port facility outside internal waters, the coastal State also has the right to take the necessary steps to prevent any breach of the conditions to which admission of those ships to internal waters or such a call is subject.
3. The coastal State may, without discrimination in form or in fact among foreign ships, suspend temporarily, in specified areas of its territorial sea, the innocent passage of foreign ships if such suspension is essential for the protection of its security, including weapons exercises. Such suspension shall take effect only after having been duly published.

ARTICLE 26

Charges which may be levied upon foreign ships

1. No charge may be levied upon foreign ships by reason only of their passage through the territorial sea.
2. Charges may be levied upon a foreign ship passing through the territorial sea as payment only for specific

services rendered to the ship. These charges shall be levied without discrimination.

Sub-Section B. *Rules Applicable to Merchant Ships and Government Ships Operated for Commercial Purposes*

ARTICLE 27

Criminal jurisdiction on board a foreign ship

1. The criminal jurisdiction of the coastal State should not be exercised on board a foreign ship passing through the territorial sea, to arrest any person or to conduct any investigation in connection with any crime committed on board the ship during its passage, save only in the following cases:
   (a) if the consequences of the crime extend to the coastal State;
   (b) if the crime is of a kind to disturb the peace of the country or the good order of the territorial sea;
   (c) if the assistance of the local authorities has been requested by the master of the ship or by a diplomatic agent or consular officer of the flag State; or
   (d) if such measures are necessary for the suppression of illicit traffic in narcotic drugs or psychotropic substances.
2. The above provisions do not affect the right of the coastal State to take any steps authorized by its laws for the purpose of making an arrest or conducting an investigation on board a foreign ship passing through the territorial sea after leaving internal waters.
3. In the cases provided for in paragraphs 1 and 2, the coastal State shall, if the master so requests, notify a diplomatic agent or consular officer of the flag State before taking any steps, and shall facilitate contact between such agent or officer and the ship's crew. In cases of emergency, this notification may be communicated while the measures are being taken.
4. In considering whether or in what manner an arrest should be made, the local authorities shall have due regard to the interests of navigation.

5. Except as provided in Part XII or with respect to violations of laws and regulations adopted in accordance with Part V, the coastal State may not take any steps on board a foreign ship passing through the territorial sea to arrest any person or to conduct any investigation in connection with any crime committed before the ship entered the territorial sea, if the ship, proceeding from a foreign port, is only passing through the territorial sea without entering internal waters.

ARTICLE 28

Civil jurisdiction in relation to foreign ships

1. The coastal State should not stop or divert a foreign ship passing through the territorial sea for the purpose of exercising civil jurisdiction in relation to a person on board the ship.
2. The coastal State may not levy execution against or arrest the ship for the purpose of any civil proceedings, save only in respect of obligations or liabilities assumed or incurred by the ship itself in the course or for the purpose of its voyage through the waters of the coastal State.
3. Paragraph 2 is without prejudice to the right of the coastal State, in accordance with its laws, to levy execution against or to arrest, for the purpose of any civil proceedings, a foreign ship lying in the territorial sea, or passing through the territorial sea after leaving internal waters.

Sub-Section C. ***Rules Applicable to Warships and Other Government Ships Operated for Non-Commercial Purposes***

ARTICLE 29

Definition of warships

For the purposes of this Convention, "warship" means a ship belonging to the armed forces of a State bearing the external marks distinguishing such a ship of its nationality, under the command of an officer duly commissioned by the government of the State and whose name appears in the appropriate service list or its equivalent, and manned by a crew which is under regular armed forces discipline.

ARTICLE 30

Non-compliance by warships with the laws and regulations of the coastal State

If any warship does not comply with the laws and regulations of the coastal State concerning passage through the territorial sea and disregards any request for compliance therewith which is made to it, the coastal State may require it to leave the territorial sea immediately.

ARTICLE 31

Responsibility of the flag State for damage caused by a warship or other government ship operated for non-commercial purposes

The flag State shall bear international responsibility for any loss or damage to the coastal State resulting from the non-compliance by a warship or other government ship operated for non-commercial purposes with the laws and regulations of the coastal State concerning passage through the territorial sea or with the provisions of this Convention or other rules of international law.

ARTICLE 32

Immunities of warships and other government ships operated for non-commercial purposes

With such exceptions as are contained in sub-section A and in articles 30 and 31, nothing in this Convention affects the immunities of warships and other government ships operated for non-commercial purposes.

SECTION 4. CONTIGUOUS ZONE

ARTICLE 33

Contiguous zone

1. In a zone contiguous to its territorial sea, described as the contiguous zone, the coastal State may exercise the control necessary to—

   (a) prevent infringement of its customs, fiscal, immigration, or sanitary laws and regulations within its territory or its territorial sea; and

(b) punish infringement of the above laws and regulations committed within its territory or its territorial sea.

2. The contiguous zone may not extend beyond 24 nautical miles from the baselines from which the breadth of the territorial sea is measured.

LAW OF SEA CONVENTION, 1982

PART-III

Straits Used for International Navigation

SECTION 1. GENERAL PROVISIONS

ARTICLE 34

Legal status of waters forming straits used for international navigation

1. The regime of passage through straits used for international navigation established in this Part shall not in other respects affect the legal status of the waters forming such straits or the exercise by the States bordering the straits of their sovereignty or jurisdiction over such waters and their air space, seabed, and subsoil.
2. The sovereignty or jurisdiction of the States bordering the straits is exercised subject to this Part and to other rules of international law.

ARTICLE 35

Scope of this Part

Nothing in this Part affects:

(a) any areas of internal waters within a strait, except where the establishment of a straight baseline in accordance with the method set forth in article 7 has the effect of enclosing as internal waters areas which had not previously been considered as such;

(b) the legal status of the waters beyond the territorial seas of States bordering straits as exclusive economic zones or high seas; or

(c) the legal regime in straits in which passage is regulated in whole or in part by long-standing international conventions in force specifically relating to such straits.

ARTICLE 36

High seas routes or routes through exclusive economic zones, through straits used for international navigation

This Part does not apply to a strait used for international navigation if there exists through the strait, a route through the high seas or through an exclusive economic zone of similar convenience with respect to navigational and hydrographical characteristics; in such routes, the other relevant Parts of this Convention, including the provisions regarding the freedoms of navigation and overflight, apply.

SECTION 2. TRANSIT PASSAGE

ARTICLE 37

Scope of this section

This section applies to straits which are used for international navigation between one part of the high seas or an exclusive economic zone and another part of the high seas or an exclusive economic zone.

ARTICLE 38

Right of transit passage

1. In straits referred to in article 37, all ships and aircraft enjoy the right of transit passage, which shall not be impeded; except that, if the strait is formed by an island of a State bordering the strait and its mainland, transit passage shall not apply if there exists, seaward of the island, a route through the high seas or through an exclusive economic zone of similar convenience with respect to navigational and hydrographical characteristics.
2. Transit passage means the exercise, in accordance with this Part, of the freedom of navigation and overflight solely for the purpose of continuous and expeditious transit of the strait between one part of the high seas or an exclusive economic zone and another part of the high seas or an exclusive economic zone. However, the requirement of continuous and expeditious transit does not preclude passage through the strait for the purpose of entering, leaving or returning from a State bordering

the strait, subject to the conditions of entry to that State.

3. Any activity which is not an exercise of the right of transit passage through a strait remains subject to the other applicable provisions of this Convention.

ARTICLE 39

Duties of ships and aircraft during transit passage

1. Ships and aircraft, while exercising the right of transit passage, shall:
   (a) proceed without delay through or over the strait;
   (b) refrain from any threat or use of force against the sovereignty, territorial integrity or political independence of States bordering the strait, or, in any other manner, violation of the principles of international law embodied in the Charter of the United Nations;
   (c) refrain from any activities other than those incident to their normal modes of continuous and expeditious transit unless rendered necessary by force *majeure* or by distress; and
   (d) comply with other relevant provisions of this Part.
2. Ships in transit passage shall:
   (a) comply with generally accepted international regulations, procedures and practices for safety at sea, including the International Regulations for Preventing Collisions at Sea; and
   (b) comply with generally accepted international regulations, procedures and practices for the prevention, reduction and control of pollution from ships.
3. Aircraft in transit passage shall:
   (a) observe the Rules of the Air established by the International Civil Aviation Organization as they apply to civil aircrafts; state aircrafts will normally comply with such safety measures and will, at all times, operate with due regard for the safety of navigation; and

(b) monitor, at all times, the radio frequency assigned by the competent internationally designated air traffic control authority or the appropriate international distress radio frequency.

ARTICLE 40

Research and survey activities

During transit passage, foreign ships, including marine scientific research and hydrographic survey ships, may not carry out any research or survey activities without the prior authorization of the States bordering straits.

ARTICLE 41

Sea lanes and traffic separation schemes in straits used for international navigation

1. In conformity with this Part, States bordering straits may designate sea lanes and prescribe traffic separation schemes for navigation in straits where necessary to promote the safe passage of ships.
2. Such States may, when circumstances require, and after giving due publicity thereto, substitute other sea lanes or traffic separation schemes for any sea lanes or traffic separation schemes previously designated or prescribed by them.
3. Such sea lanes and traffic separation schemes shall conform to generally accepted international regulations.
4. Before designating or substituting sea lanes or prescribing or substituting traffic separation schemes, States bordering straits shall refer proposals to the competent international organization with a view to their adoption. The organization may adopt only such sea lanes and traffic separation schemes as may be agreed with the States bordering the straits, after which the States may designate, prescribe or substitute them.
5. In respect of a strait where sea lanes or traffic separation schemes through the waters of two or more States bordering the strait are being proposed, the States concerned shall cooperate in formulating proposals in consultation with the competent international organization.

6. States bordering straits shall clearly indicate all sea lanes and traffic separation schemes designated or prescribed by them on charts to which due publicity shall be given.
7. Ships in transit passage shall respect applicable sea lanes and traffic separation schemes established in accordance with this article.

ARTICLE 42

Laws and regulations of States bordering straits relating to transit passage

1. Subject to the provisions of this section, States bordering straits may adopt laws and regulations relating to transit passage through straits, in respect of all or any of the following:
   (a) the safety of navigation and the regulation of maritime traffic, as provided in article 41;
   (b) the prevention, reduction and control of pollution, by giving effect to applicable international regulations regarding the discharge of oil, oily wastes and other noxious substances in the strait;
   (c) with respect to fishing vessels, the prevention of fishing, including the stowage of fishing gear; or
   (d) the loading or unloading of any commodity, currency or person in contravention of the customs, fiscal, immigration or sanitary laws and regulations of States bordering straits.
2. Such laws and regulations shall not discriminate in form or in fact among foreign ships or in their application have the practical effect of denying, hampering or impairing the right of transit passage as defined in this section.
3. States bordering straits shall give due publicity to all such laws and regulations.
4. Foreign ships exercising the right of transit passage shall comply with such laws and regulations.
5. The flag State of a ship or the State of registry of an aircraft entitled to sovereign immunity which acts in a manner contrary to such laws and regulations or other

provisions of this Part shall bear international responsibility for any loss or damage which results to States bordering straits.

ARTICLE 43

Navigational and safety aids and other improvements and the prevention, reduction and control of pollution

User States and States bordering a strait should by agreement cooperate:

(a) in the establishment and maintenance, in a strait of necessary navigational and safety aids or other improvements in aid of international navigation; and

(b) for the prevention, reduction and control of pollution from ships.

ARTICLE 44

Duties of states bordering straits

States bordering straits shall not hamper transit passage and shall give appropriate publicity to any danger to navigation or overflight within or over the strait of which they have knowledge. There shall be no suspension of transit passage.

SECTION 3. INNOCENT PASSAGE

ARTICLE 45

Innocent passage

1. The regime of innocent passage, in accordance with Part II, section 3, shall apply in straits used for international navigation:
   (a) excluded from the application of the regime of transit passage under article 38, paragraph 1; or
   (b) between a part of the high seas or an exclusive economic zone and the territorial sea of a foreign State.
2. There shall be no suspension of innocent passage through such straits.

LAW OF SEA CONVENTION, 1982

PART-IV

Archipelagic State

ARTICLE 46

Use of terms

For the purposes of this Convention:

(a) "archipelagic State" means a State constituted wholly by one or more archipelagos and may include other islands; and

(b) "archipelago" means a group of islands, including parts of islands, interconnecting waters and other natural features which are so closely interrelated that such islands, waters and other natural features form an intrinsic geographical, economic and political entity, or which historically have been regarded as such.

ARTICLE 47

Archipelagic baselines

1. An archipelagic State may draw straight archipelagic baselines joining the outermost points of the outermost islands and drying reefs of the archipelago, provided that within such baselines are included the main islands and an area in which the ratio of the area of the water to the area of the land, including atolls, is between 1 to 1 and 9 to 1.
2. The length of such baselines shall not exceed 100 nautical miles, except that up to 3 per cent of the total number of baselines enclosing any archipelago may exceed that length, up to a maximum length of 125 nautical miles.
3. The drawing of such baselines shall not depart to any appreciable extent from the general configuration of the archipelago.
4. Such baselines shall not be drawn to and from low-tide elevations, unless lighthouses or similar installations

which are permanently above sea level have been built on them or where a low-tide elevation is situated wholly or partly at a distance not exceeding the breadth of the territorial sea from the nearest island.

5. The system of such baselines shall not be applied by an archipelagic State in such a manner as to cut off from the high seas or the exclusive economic zone the territorial sea of another State.
6. If a part of the archipelagic waters of an archipelagic State lies between two parts of an immediately adjacent neighbouring State, existing rights and all other legitimate interests which the latter State has traditionally exercised in such waters and all rights stipulated by agreement between those States shall continue and be respected.
7. For the purpose of computing the ratio of water to land under paragraph 1, land areas may include waters lying within the fringing reefs of islands and atolls, including that part of a steep-sided oceanic plateau which is enclosed or nearly enclosed by a chain of limestone islands and drying reefs lying on the perimeter of the plateau.
8. The baselines drawn, in accordance with this article, shall be shown on charts of a scale or scales adequate for ascertaining their position. Alternatively, lists of geographical coordinates of points, specifying the geodetic datum, may be substituted.
9. The archipelagic State shall give due publicity to such charts or lists of geographical coordinates, and shall deposit a copy of each such chart or list with the Secretary-General of the United Nations.

ARTICLE 48

Measurement of the breadth of the territorial sea, the contiguous zone, the exclusive economic zone and the continental shelf

The breadth of the territorial sea, the contiguous zone, the exclusive economic zone and the continental shelf shall be measured from archipelagic baselines drawn in accordance with article 47.

ARTICLE 49

Legal status of archipelagic waters, of the air space over archipelagic waters and of their bed and subsoil

1. The sovereignty of an archipelagic State extends to the waters enclosed by the archipelagic baselines drawn in accordance with article 47, described as archipelagic waters, regardless of their depth or distance from the coast.
2. This sovereignty extends to the air space over the archipelagic waters, as well as to their bed and subsoil, and the resources contained therein.
3. This sovereignty is exercised subject to this Part.
4. The regime of archipelagic sea lanes passage established in this Part shall not in other respects affect the status of the archipelagic waters, including the sea lanes, or the exercise by the archipelagic State of its sovereignty over such waters and their air space, bed and subsoil, and the resources contained therein.

ARTICLE 50

Delimitation of internal waters

Within its archipelagic waters, the archipelagic State may draw closing lines for the delimitation of internal waters, in accordance with articles 9, 10 and 11.

ARTICLE 51

Existing agreements, traditional fishing rights and existing submarine cables

1. Without prejudice to article 49, an archipelagic State shall respect existing agreements with other States and shall recognize traditional fishing rights and other legitimate activities of the immediately adjacent neighbouring States in certain areas falling within archipelagic waters. The terms and conditions for the exercise of such rights and activities, including the nature, the extent and the areas to which they apply, shall, at the request of any of the States concerned, be regulated by bilateral agreements between them. Such

rights shall not be transferred to or shared with third States or their nationals.

2. An archipelagic State shall respect existing submarine cables laid by other States and passing through its waters without making a landfall. An archipelagic State shall permit the maintenance and replacement of such cables upon receiving due notice of their location and the intention to repair or replace them.

ARTICLE 52

Right of innocent passage

1. Subject to article 53 and without prejudice to article 50, ships of all States enjoy the right of innocent passage through archipelagic waters, in accordance with Part II, section 3.
2. The archipelagic State may, without discrimination in form or in fact among foreign ships, suspend temporarily in specified areas of its archipelagic waters, the innocent passage of foreign ships if such suspension is essential for the protection of its security. Such suspension shall take effect only after having been duly published.

ARTICLE 53

Right of archipelagic sea lanes passage

1. An archipelagic State may designate sea lanes and air routes thereabove, suitable for the continuous and expeditious passage of foreign ships and aircraft, through or over its archipelagic waters and the adjacent territorial sea.
2. All ships and aircraft enjoy the right of archipelagic sea lanes passage in such sea lanes and air routes.
3. Archipelagic sea lanes passage means the exercise, in accordance with this Convention, of the rights of navigation and overflight in the normal mode solely for the purpose of continuous, expeditious and unobstructed transit between one part of the high seas or an exclusive economic zone and another part of the high seas or an exclusive economic zone.

4. Such sea lanes and air routes shall traverse the archipelagic waters and the adjacent territorial sea and shall include all normal passage routes used as routes for international navigation or overflight through or over archipelagic waters and, within such routes, so far as ships are concerned, all normal navigational channels, provided that duplication of routes of similar convenience between the same entry and exit points shall not be necessary.
5. Such sea lanes and air routes shall be defined by a series of continuous axis lines from the entry points of passage routes to the exit points. Ships and aircraft in archipelagic sea lanes passage shall not deviate more than 25 nautical miles to either side of such axis lines during passage, provided that such ships and aircraft shall not navigate closer to the coasts than 10 per cent of the distance between the nearest points on islands bordering the sea lane.
6. An archipelagic State which designates sea lanes under this article may also prescribe traffic separation schemes for the safe passage of ships through narrow channels in such sea lanes.
7. An archipelagic State may, when circumstances require, after giving due publicity thereto, substitute other sea lanes or traffic separation schemes for any sea lanes or traffic separation schemes previously designated or prescribed by it.
8. Such sea lanes and traffic separation schemes shall conform to generally accepted international regulations.
9. In designating or substituting sea lanes or prescribing or substituting traffic separation schemes, an archipelagic State shall refer proposals to the competent international organization with a view to their adoption. The organization may adopt only such sea lanes and traffic separation schemes as may be agreed with the archipelagic State, after which the archipelagic State may designate, prescribe or substitute them.
10. The archipelagic State shall clearly indicate the axis of the sea lanes and the traffic separation schemes

designated or prescribed by it on charts to which due publicity shall be given.

11. Ships in archipelagic sea lanes passage shall respect applicable sea lanes and traffic separation schemes established in accordance with this article.

12. If an archipelagic State does not designate sea lanes or air routes, the right of archipelagic sea lanes passage may be exercised through the routes normally used for international navigation.

ARTICLE 54

Duties of ships and aircraft during their passage, research and survey activities and duties laws and regulations of the archipelagic State relating to archipelagic sea lanes passage

Articles 39, 40, 42 and 44 apply *mutatis mutandis* to archipelagic sea lanes passage.

LAW OF SEA CONVENTION, 1982

PART-V

EXCLUSIVE ECONOMIC ZONE

ARTICLE 55

Specific legal regime of the exclusive economic zone

The exclusive economic zone is an area beyond and adjacent to the territorial sea, subject to the specific legal regime established in this Part, under which the rights and jurisdiction of the coastal State and the rights and freedoms of other States are governed by the relevant provisions of this Convention.

ARTICLE 56

Rights, jurisdiction and duties of the coastal State in the exclusive economic zone

1. In the exclusive economic zone, the coastal State has:
   (a) sovereign rights for the purpose of exploring and exploiting, conserving and managing the natural resources, whether living or non-living, of the waters superjacent to the seabed and of the seabed and its subsoil, and with regard to other activities for the economic exploitation and exploration of the zone, such as the production of energy from the water, currents and winds; and
   (b) jurisdiction, as provided for in the relevant provisions of this Convention, with regard to —
      (i) the establishment and use of artificial islands, installations and structures,
      (ii) the marine scientific research,
      (iii) the protection and preservation of the marine environment, and
   (c) other rights and duties provided for in this Convention.
2. In exercising its rights and performing its duties under this Convention in the exclusive economic zone, the

coastal State shall have due regard to the rights and duties of other States, and shall act in a manner compatible with the provisions of this Convention.

3. The rights set out in this article with respect to the seabed and the subsoil shall be exercised in accordance with Part VI.

ARTICLE 57

Breadth of the exclusive economic zone

The exclusive economic zone shall not extend beyond 200 nautical miles from the baselines from which the breadth of the territorial sea is measured.

ARTICLE 58

Rights and duties of other States in the exclusive economic zone

1. In the exclusive economic zone, all States, whether coastal or landlocked, enjoy, subject to the relevant provisions of this Convention, the freedoms referred to in article 87 of navigation and overflight and of the laying of submarine cables and pipelines, and other internationally lawful uses of the sea related to these freedoms, such as those associated with the operation of ships, aircraft, and submarine cables and pipelines, and compatible with the other provisions of this Convention.
2. Articles 88 to 115 and other pertinent rules of international law apply to the exclusive economic zone in so far as they are not incompatible with this Part.
3. In exercising their rights and performing their duties under this Convention in the exclusive economic zone, States shall have due regard to the rights and duties of the coastal State, and shall comply with the laws and regulations adopted by the coastal State in accordance with the provisions of this Convention and other rules of international law in so far as they are not incompatible with this Part.

ARTICLE 59

Basis for the resolution of conflicts regarding the attribution of rights and jurisdiction in the exclusive economic zone

In cases where this Convention does not attribute rights or jurisdiction to the coastal State or to other States within the exclusive economic zone, and a conflict arises between the interests of the coastal State and any other State or States, the conflict should be resolved on the basis of equity and in the light of all the relevant circumstances, taking into account the respective importance of the interests involved of the parties as well as of the international community as a whole.

ARTICLE 60

Artificial islands, installations and structures in the exclusive economic zone

1. In the exclusive economic zone, the coastal State shall have the exclusive right to construct and to authorize and to regulate the construction, operation and use of —
   (a) artificial islands;
   (b) installations and structures for the purposes provided for in article 56 and other economic purposes; and
   (c) installations and structures which may interfere with the exercise of the rights of the coastal State in the zone.
2. The coastal State shall have exclusive jurisdiction over such artificial islands, installations and structures, including jurisdiction with regard to customs, fiscal, health, safety and immigration laws and regulations.
3. Due notice must be given of the construction of such artificial islands, installations or structures, and permanent means for giving warning of their presence must be maintained. Any installations or structures which are abandoned or disused shall be removed to ensure safety of navigation, taking into account any generally accepted international standards established in this regard by the competent international organization. Such removal shall also have due regard

to fishing, the protection of the marine environment and the rights and duties of other States. Appropriate publicity shall be given to the depth, position and dimensions of any installations or structures not entirely removed.

4. The coastal State may, where necessary, establish reasonable safety zones around such artificial islands, installations and structures in which it may take appropriate measures to ensure the safety both of navigation and of the artificial islands, installations and structures.
5. The breadth of the safety zones shall be determined by the coastal State, taking into account applicable international standards. Such zones shall be designed to ensure that they are reasonably related to the nature and function of the artificial islands, installations or structures, and shall not exceed a distance of 500 metres around them, measured from each point of their outer edge, except as authorized by generally accepted international standards or as recommended by the competent international organization. Due notice shall be given of the extent of safety zones.
6. All ships must respect these safety zones and shall comply with generally accepted international standards regarding navigation in the vicinity of artificial islands, installations, structures and safety zones.
7. Artificial islands, installations and structures and the safety zones around them may not be established where interference may be caused to the use of recognized sea lanes essential to international navigation.
8. Artificial islands, installations and structures do not possess the status of islands. They have no territorial sea of their own, and their presence does not affect the delimitation of the territorial sea, the exclusive economic zone or the continenal shelf.

ARTICLE 61

Conservation of the living resources

1. The coastal State shall determine the allowable catch of the living resources in its exclusive economic zone.

2. The coastal State, taking into account the best scientific evidence available to it, shall ensure, through proper conservation and management measures, that the maintenance of the living resources in the exclusive economic zone is not endangered by over-exploitation. As appropriate, the coastal State and the competent international organizations, whether subregional, regional or global, shall cooperate to this end.
3. Such measures shall also be designed to maintain or to restore populations of harvested species at levels which can produce the maximum sustainable yield, as qualified by relevant environmental and economic factors, including the economic needs of coastal fishing communities and the special requirements of developing States, and taking into account fishing patterns, the interdependence of stocks and any generally recommended international minimum standards, whether subregional, regional or global.
4. In taking such measures the coastal State shall take into consideration, the effects on species associated with or dependent upon harvested species with a view to maintain or to restore populations of such associated or dependent species above levels at which their reproduction may become seriously threatened.
5. Available scientific information, catch and fishing effort statistics, and other data relevant to the conservation of fish stocks shall be contributed and exchanged on a regular basis through competent international organizations, whether subregional, regional or global, where appropriate and with participation by all States concerned, including States whose nationals are allowed to fish in the exclusive economic zone.

ARTICLE 62

Utilization of the living resources

1. The coastal State shall promote the objective of optimum utilization of the living resources in the exclusive economic zone without prejudice to article 61.
2. The coastal State shall determine its capacity to harvest the living resources of the exclusive economic zone.

Where the coastal State does not have the capacity to harvest the entire allowable catch, it shall, through agreements or other arrangements and pursuant to the terms, conditions, laws and regulations referred to in paragraph 4, give other States access to the surplus of the allowable catch, having particular regard to the provisions of articles 69 and 70, especially in relation to the developing States mentioned therein.

3. In giving access to other States to its exclusive economic zone under this article, the coastal State shall take into account all relevant factors, including, *inter alia*, the significance of the living resources of the area to the economy of the coastal State concerned and its other national interests, the provisions of articles 69 and 70, the requirements of developing States in the subregion or region in harvesting part of the surplus and the need to minimize economic dislocation in States whose nationals have habitually fished in the zone or which have made substantial efforts in research and identification of stocks.

4. Nationals of other States fishing in the exclusive economic zone shall comply with the conservation measures and with the other terms and conditions established in the laws and regulations of the coastal State. These laws and regulations shall be consistent with this Convention and may relate, *inter alia*, to the following:

   (a) licensing of fishermen, fishing vessels and equipment, including payment of fees and other forms of remuneration, which, in the case of developing coastal States, may consist of adequate compensation in the field of financing, equipment and technology relating to the fishing industry;

   (b) determining the species which may be caught, and fixing quotas of catch, whether in relation to particular stocks or groups of stocks or catch per vessel over a period of time or to the catch by nationals of any State during a specified period;

   (c) regulating seasons and areas of fishing, the types, sizes and amount of gear, and the types, sizes and number of fishing vessels that may be used;

(d) fixing the age and size of fish and other species that may be caught;

(e) specifying information required of fishing vessels, including catch and effort statistics and vessel position reports;

(f) requiring, under the authorization and control of the coastal State, the conduct of specified fisheries research programmes and regulating the conduct of such research, including the sampling of catches, disposition of samples and reporting of associated scientific data;

(g) the placing of observers or trainees on board such vessels by the coastal State;

(h) the landing of all or any part of the catch by such vessels in the ports of the coastal State;

(i) terms and conditions relating to joint ventures or other cooperative arrangements;

(j) requirements for the training of personnel and the transfer of fisheries technology, including enhancement of the coastal State's capability of undertaking fisheries research;

(k) enforcement procedures.

5. Coastal States shall give due notice of conservation and management laws and regulations.

ARTICLE 63

Stocks occurring within the exclusive economic zones of two or more coastal States or both within the exclusive economic zone and in an area beyond and adjacent to it

1. Where the same stock or stocks of associated species occur within the exclusive economic zones of two or more coastal States, these States shall seek, either directly or through appropriate subregional or regional organizations, to agree upon the measures necessary to coordinate and ensure the conservation and development of such stocks without prejudice to the other provisions of this Part.

2. Where the same stock or stocks of associated species occur both within the exclusive economic zone and in

an area beyond and adjacent to the zone, the coastal State and the States fishing for such stocks in the adjacent area shall seek, either directly or through appropriate subregional or regional organizations, to agree upon the measures necessary for the conservation of these stocks in the adjacent area.

ARTICLE 64

Highly migratory species

1. The coastal State and other States whose nationals fish in the region for the highly migratory species, listed in Annex I, shall cooperate directly or through appropriate international organizations with a view to ensuring conservation and promoting the objective of optimum utilization of such species throughout the region, both within and beyond the exclusive economic zone. In regions for which no appropriate international organization exists, the coastal State and other States whose nationals harvest these species in the region shall cooperate to establish such an organization and participate in its work.
2. The provisions of paragraph 1 apply in addition to the other provisions of this Part.

ARTICLE 65

Marine mammals

Nothing in this Part restricts the right of a coastal State or the competence of an international organization, as appropriate, to prohibit, limit or regulate the exploitation of marine mammals more strictly than provided for in this Part. States shall cooperate with a view to the conservation of marine mammals and in the case of cetaceans shall, in particular, work through the appropriate international organizations for their conservation, management and study.

ARTICLE 66

Anadromous stocks

1. States in whose rivers anadromous stocks originate shall have the primary interest in and responsibility for such stocks.

2. The State of origin of anadromous stocks shall ensure their conservation by the establishment of appropriate regulatory measures for fishing in all waters landward of the outer limits of its exclusive economic zone and for fishing provided for in paragraph 3(b). The State of origin may, after consultations with the other States referred to in paragraphs 3 and 4 fishing these stocks, establish total allowable catches for stocks originating in its rivers.

3. (a) Fisheries for anadromous stocks shall be conducted only in waters landward of the outer limits of exclusive economic zones, except in cases where this provision would result in economic dislocation for a State other than the State of origin. With respect to such fishing beyond the outer limits of the exclusive economic zone, States concerned shall maintain consultations with a view to achieving agreement on terms and conditions of such fishing, giving due regard to the conservation requirements and the needs of the State of origin in respect of these stocks.

(b) The State of origin shall cooperate in minimizing economic dislocation in such other States fishing these stocks, taking into account the normal catch and the mode of operations of such States, and all the areas in which such fishing has occurred.

(c) States referred to in subparagraph (b), participating by agreement with the State of origin in measures to renew anadromous stocks, particularly by expenditures for that purpose, shall be given special consideration by the State of origin in the harvesting of stocks originating in its rivers.

(d) Enforcement of regulations regarding anadromous stocks beyond the exclusive economic zone shall be, by agreement, between the State of origin and the other States concerned.

4. In cases where anadromous stocks migrate into or through the waters landward of the outer limits of the exclusive economic zone of a State other than the State

of origin, such State shall cooperate with the State of origin with regard to the conservation and management of such stocks.

5. The State of origin of anadromous stocks and other States fishing these stocks shall make arrangements for the implementation of the provisions of this article, where appropriate, through regional organizations.

ARTICLE 67

Catadromous species

1. A coastal State in whose waters catadromous species spend the greater part of their life cycle shall have responsibility for the management of these species and shall ensure the ingress and egress of migrating fish.
2. Harvesting of catadromous species shall be conducted only in waters landward of the outer limits of exclusive economic zones. When conducted in exclusive economic zones, harvesting shall be subject to this article and the other provisions of this Convention concerning fishing in these zones.
3. In cases where catadromous fish migrate through the exclusive economic zone of another State, whether as juvenile or maturing fish, the management, including harvesting, of such fish shall be regulated by agreement between the State mentioned in paragraph 1 and the other State concerned. Such agreement shall ensure the rational management of the species and take into account the responsibilities of the State mentioned in paragraph 1 for the maintenance of these species.

ARTICLE 68

Sedentary species

This Part does not apply to sedentary species as defined in article 77, paragraph 4.

ARTICLE 69

Right of landlocked States

1. Landlocked States shall have the right to participate, on an equitable basis, in the exploitation of an appropriate

part of the surplus of the living resources of the exclusive economic zones of coastal States of the same subregion or region, taking into account the relevant economic and geographical circumstances of all the States concerned and in conformity with the provisions of this article and of articles 61 and 62.

2. The terms and modalities of such participation shall be established by the States concerned through bilateral, subregional or regional agreements taking into account, *inter alia*:
   (a) the need to avoid effects detrimental to fishing communities or fishing industries of the coastal State;
   (b) the extent to which the landlocked State, in accordance with the provisions of this article, is participating or is entitled to participate under existing bilateral, subregional or regional agreements in the exploitation of living resources of the exclusive economic zones of other coastal States;
   (c) the extent to which other landlocked States and geographically disadvantaged States are participating in the exploitation of the living resources of the exclusive economic zone of the coastal State, and the consequent need to avoid a particular burden for any single coastal State or a part of it; and
   (d) the nutritional needs of the populations of the respective States.

3. When the harvesting capacity of a coastal State approaches a point which would enable it to harvest the entire allowable catch of the living resources in its exclusive economic zone, the coastal State and other States concerned shall cooperate in the establishment of equitable arrangements on a bilateral, subregional or regional basis to allow for participation of developing landlocked States of the same subregion or region in the exploitation of the living resources of the exclusive economic zones of coastal States of the subregion or

region, as may be appropriate in the circumstances and on terms satisfactory to all parties. In the implementation of this provision the factors mentioned in paragraph 2 shall also be taken into account.

4. Developed landlocked States shall, under the provisions of this article, be entitled to participate in the exploitation of living resources only in the exclusive economic zones of developed coastal States of the same subregion or region having regard to the extent to which the coastal State, in giving access to other States to the living resources of its exclusive economic zone, has taken into account the need to minimize detrimental effects on fishing communities and economic dislocation in States whose nationals have habitually fished in the zone.

5. The above provisions are without prejudice to arrangements agreed upon in subregions or regions where the coastal States may grant to landlocked States of the same subregion or region equal or preferential rights for the exploitation of the living resources in the exclusive economic zones.

ARTICLE 70

Right of geographically disadvantaged States

1. Geographically disadvantaged States shall have the right to participate, on an equitable basis, in the exploitation of an appropriate part of the surplus of the living resources of the exclusive economic zones of coastal States of the same subregion or region, taking into account the relevant economic and geographical circumstances of all the States concerned and in conformity with the provisions of this article and of articles 61 and 62.

2. For the purposes of this Part, "geographically disadvantaged States" mean coastal States, including States bordering enclosed or semi-enclosed seas, whose geographical situation makes them dependent upon the exploitation of the living resources of the exclusive economic zones of other States in the subregion or region for adequate supplies of fish for the nutritional

purposes of their populations or parts thereof, and coastal States which can claim no exclusive economic zones of their own.

3. The terms and modalities of such participation shall be established by the States concerned through bilateral, subregional or regional agreements taking into account, *inter alia*:

   (a) the need to avoid effects detrimental to fishing communities or fishing industries of the coastal State;

   (b) the extent to which the geographically disadvantaged State, in accordance with the provisions of this article, is participating or is entitled to participate under existing bilateral, subregional or regional agreements in the exploitation of living resources of the exclusive economic zones of other coastal States;

   (c) the extent to which other geographically disadvantaged States and landlocked States are participating in the exploitation of the living resources of the exclusive economic zone of the coastal State and the consequent need to avoid a particular burden for any single coastal State or a part of it; and

   (d) the nutritional needs of the populations of the respective States.

4. When the harvesting capacity of a coastal State approaches a point which would enable it to harvest the entire allowable catch of the living resources in its exclusive economic zone, the coastal State and other States concerned shall cooperate in the establishment of equitable arrangements on a bilateral, subregional or regional basis to allow for participation of developing geographically disadvantaged States of the same subregion or region in the exploitation of the living resources of the exclusive economic zones of coastal States of the subregion or region, as may be appropriate in the circumstances and on terms satisfactory to all parties. In the implementation of this provision the

factors mentioned in paragraph 3 shall also be taken into account.

5. Developed geographically disadvantaged States shall, under the provisions of this article, be entitled to participate in the exploitation of living resources only in the exclusive economic zones of developed coastal States of the same subregion or region having regard to the extent to which the coastal State, in giving access to other States to the living resources of its exclusive economic zone, has taken into account the need to minimize detrimental effects on fishing communities and economic dislocation in States whose nationals have habitually fished in the zone.

6. The above provisions are without prejudice to arrangements agreed upon in subregions or regions where the coastal States may grant to geographically disadvantaged States of the same subregion or region, equal or preferential rights for the exploitation of the living resources in the exclusive economic zones.

ARTICLE 71

Non-applicability of articles 69 and 70

The provisions of articles 69 and 70 do not apply in the case of a coastal State whose economy is overwhelmingly dependent on the exploitation of the living resources of its exclusive economic zone.

ARTICLE 72

Restrictions on transfer of rights

1. Rights provided under articles 69 and 70 to exploit living resources shall not be directly or indirectly transferred to third States or their nationals by lease or licence, by establishing joint ventures or in any other manner which has the effect of such transfer, unless otherwise agreed by the States concerned.

2. The foregoing provision does not preclude the States concerned from obtaining technical or financial assistance from third States or international organizations in order to facilitate the exercise of the

rights pursuant to articles 69 and 70, provided that it does not have the effect referred to in paragraph 1.

ARTICLE 73

Enforcement of laws and regulations of the coastal State

1. The coastal State may, in the exercise of its sovereign rights to explore, exploit, conserve and manage the living resources in the exclusive economic zone, take such measures, including boarding, inspection, arrest and judicial proceedings, as may be necessary to ensure compliance with the laws and regulations adopted by it in conformity with this Convention.
2. Arrested vessels and their crews shall be promptly released upon the posting of reasonable bond or other security.
3. Coastal State penalties for violations of fisheries laws and regulations in the exclusive economic zone may not include imprisonment, in the absence of agreements to the contrary by the States concerned, or any other form of corporal punishment.
4. In cases of arrest or detention of foreign vessels, the coastal State shall promptly notify the flag State, through appropriate channels, of the action taken and of any penalties subsequently imposed.

ARTICLE 74

Delimitation of the exclusive economic zone between States with opposite or adjacent coasts

1. The delimitation of the exclusive economic zone between States with opposite or adjacent coasts shall be effected by agreement on the basis of international law, as referred to in Article 38 of the Statute of the International Court of Justice, in order to achieve an equitable solution.
2. If no agreement can be reached within a reasonable period of time, the States concerned shall resort to the procedures provided for in Part XV.
3. Pending agreement, as provided for in paragraph 1, the States concerned, in a spirit of understanding and cooperation, shall make every effort to enter into

provisional arrangements of a practical nature and, during this transitional period, not to jeopardize or hamper the reaching of the final agreement. Such arrangements shall be without prejudice to the final delimitation.

4. Where there is an agreement in force between the States concerned, questions relating to the delimitation of the exclusive economic zone shall be determined in accordance with the provisions of that agreement.

ARTICLE 75

Charts and lists of geographical coordinates

1. Subject to this Part, the outer limit lines of the exclusive economic zone and the lines of delimitation drawn in accordance with article 74 shall be shown on charts of a scale or scales adequate for ascertaining their position. Where appropriate, lists of geographical coordinates of points, specifying the geodetic datum, may be substituted for such outer limit lines or lines of delimitation.
2. The coastal State shall give due publicity to such charts or lists of geographical coordinates and shall deposit a copy of each such chart or list with the Secretary-General of the United Nations.

LAW OF SEA CONVENTION, 1982

PART-VI

CONTINENTAL SHELF

ARTICLE 76

Definition of the continental shelf

1. The continental shelf of a coastal State comprises the seabed and subsoil of the submarine areas that extend beyond its territorial sea throughout the natural prolongation of its land territory, to the outer edge of the continental margin, or to a distance of 200 nautical miles from the baselines from which the breadth of the territorial sea is measured, where the outer edge of the continental margin does not extend up to that distance.
2. The continental shelf of a coastal State shall not extend beyond the limits provided for in paragraphs 4 to 6.
3. The continental margin comprises the submerged prolongation of the land mass of the coastal State, and consists of the seabed and subsoil of the shelf, the slope and the rise. It does not include the deep ocean-floor with its oceanic ridges or the subsoil thereof.
4. (a) For the purposes of this Convention, the coastal State shall establish the outer edge of the continental margin wherever the margin extends beyond 200 nautical miles from the baselines from which the breadth of the territorial sea is measured, by either:
   - (i) a line delineated, in accordance with paragraph 7, by reference to the outermost fixed points at each of which the thickness of sedimentary rocks is at least 1 per cent of the shortest distance from such point to the foot of the continental slope; or
   - (ii) a line delineated in accordance with paragraph 7 by reference to fixed points not more than 60 nautical miles from the foot of the continental slope.

(b) In the absence of evidence to the contrary, the foot of the continental slope shall be determined as the point of maximum change in the gradient at its base.

5. The fixed points comprising the line of the outer limits of the continental shelf on the seabed, drawn in accordance with paragraph 4 (a)(i) and (ii), either shall not exceed 350 nautical miles from the baselines from which the breadth of the territorial sea is measured or shall not exceed 100 nautical miles from the 2,500 metre isobath, which is a line connecting the depth of 2,500 metres.

6. Notwithstanding the provisions of paragraph 5, on submarine ridges, the outer limit of the continental shelf shall not exceed 350 nautical miles from the baselines from which the breadth of the territorial sea is measured. This paragraph does not apply to submarine elevations that are natural components of the continental margin, such as its plateaux, rises, caps, banks and spurs.

7. The coastal State shall delineate the outer limits of its continental shelf, where that shelf extends beyond 200 nautical miles from the baselines from which the breadth of the territorial sea is measured, by straight-lines not exceeding 60 nautical miles in length, connecting fixed points, defined by coordinates of latitude and longitude.

8. Information on the limits of the continental shelf beyond 200 nautical miles from the baselines from which the breadth of the territorial sea is measured, shall be submitted by the coastal State to the Commission on the limits of the Continental Shelf set up under Annex II on the basis of equitable geographical representation. The Commission shall make recommendations to coastal States on matters related to the establishment of the outer limits of their continental shelf. The limits of the shelf established by a coastal State on the basis of these recommendations shall be final and binding.

9. The coastal State shall deposit with the Secretary-General of the United Nations charts and relevant information, including geodetic data, permanently describing the outer limits of its continental shelf. The Secretary-General shall give due publicity thereto.
10. The provisions of this article are without prejudice to the question of delimitation of the continental shelf between States with opposite or adjacent coasts.

ARTICLE 77

Rights of the coastal State over the continental shelf

1. The coastal State exercises over the continental shelf sovereign rights for the purpose of exploring it and exploiting its natural resources.
2. The rights referred to in paragraph 1 are exclusive in the sense that if the coastal State does not explore the continental shelf or exploit its natural resources, no one may undertake these activities without the express consent of the coastal State.
3. The rights of the coastal State over the continental shelf do not depend on occupation, effective or notional, or on any express proclamation.
4. The natural resources referred to in this Part consist of the mineral and other non-living resources of the seabed and the subsoil together with living organisms belonging to sedentary species, that is to say, organisms which, at the harvestable stage, either are immobile on or under the seabed or are unable to move except in constant physical contact with the seabed or the subsoil.

ARTICLE 78

Legal status of the superjacent waters and air space and the rights and freedoms of other States

1. The rights of the coastal State over the continental shelf do not affect the legal status of the superjacent waters or of the air space above those waters.
2. The exercise of the rights of the coastal State over the continental shelf must not infringe or result in any unjustifiable interference with navigation and other

rights and freedoms of other States as provided for in this Convention.

ARTICLE 79

Submarine cables and pipelines on the continental shelf

1. All States are entitled to lay submarine cables and pipelines on the continental shelf, in accordance with the provisions of this article.
2. Subject to its right to take reasonable measures for the exploration of the continental shelf, the exploitation of its natural resources and the prevention, reduction and control of pollution from pipelines, the coastal State may not impede the laying or maintenance of such cables or pipelines.
3. The delineation of the course for the laying of such pipelines on the continental shelf is subject to the consent of the coastal State.
4. Nothing in this Part affects the right of the coastal State to establish conditions for cables or pipelines entering its territory or territorial sea, or its jurisdiction over cables and pipelines constructed or used in connection with the exploration of its continental shelf or exploitation of its resources or the operations of artificial islands, installations and structures under its jurisdiction.
5. When laying submarine cables or pipelines, States shall have due regard to cables or pipelines already in position. In particular, possibilities of repairing existing cables or pipelines shall not be prejudiced.

ARTICLE 80

Artificial islands, installations and structures on the continental shelf

Article 60 applies *mutatis mutandis* to artificial islands, installations and structures on the continental shelf.

ARTICLE 81

Drilling on the continental shelf

The coastal State shall have the exclusive right to authorize and regulate drilling on the continental shelf for all purposes.

ARTICLE 82

Payments and contributions with respect to the exploitation of the continental shelf beyond 200 nautical miles

1. The coastal State shall make payments or contributions in kind, in respect of the exploitation of the non-living resources of the continental shelf beyond 200 nautical miles from the baselines from which the breadth of the territorial sea is measured.
2. The payments and contributions shall be made annually with respect to all production at a site after the first five years of production at that site. For the sixth year, the rate of payment or contribution shall be 1 per cent of the value or volume of production at the site. The rate shall increase by 1 per cent for each subsequent year until the twelfth year and shall remain at 7 per cent thereafter. Production does not include resources used in connection with exploitation.
3. A developing State which is a net importer of a mineral resource produced from its continental shelf is exempt from making such payments or contributions in respect of that mineral resource.
4. The payments or contributions shall be made through the Authority, which shall distribute them to States Parties to this Convention, on the basis of equitable sharing criteria, taking into account the interests and needs of developing States, particularly the least developed and the landlocked among them.

ARTICLE 83

Delimitation of the continental shelf between States with opposite or adjacent coasts

1. The delimitation of the continental shelf between States with opposite or adjacent coasts shall be effected by agreement on the basis of international law, as referred to in Article 38 of the Statute of the International Court of Justice, in order to achieve an equitable solution.
2. If no agreement can be reached within a reasonable period of time, the States concerned shall resort to the procedures provided for in Part XV.

3. Pending agreement as provided for in paragraph 1, the States concerned, in a spirit of understanding and cooperation, shall make every effort to enter into provisional arrangements of a practical nature and, during this transitional period, not to jeopardize or hamper the reaching of the final agreement. Such arrangements shall be without prejudice to the final delimitation.
4. Where there is an agreement in force between the States concerned, questions relating to the delimitation of the continental shelf shall be determined in accordance with the provisions of that agreement.

ARTICLE 84

Charts and lists of geographical coordinates

1. Subject to this Part, the outer limit lines of the continental shelf and the lines of delimitation drawn in accordance with article 83 shall be shown on charts of a scale or scales adequate for ascertaining their position. Where appropriate, lists of geographical coordinates of points, specifying the geodetic datum, may be substituted for such outer limit lines or lines of delimitation.
2. The coastal State shall give due publicity to such charts or lists of geographical coordinates and shall deposit a copy of each such chart or list with the Secretary-General of the United Nations and, in the case of those showing the outer limit lines of the continental shelf, with the Secretary-General of the Authority.

ARTICLE 85

Tunnelling

This Part does not prejudice the right of the coastal State to exploit the subsoil by means of tunnelling, irrespective of the depth of water above the subsoil.

LAW OF SEA CONVENTION, 1982

PART-VII

High Seas

SECTION 1. GENERAL PROVISIONS

ARTICLE 86

Application of the provisions of this Part

The provisions of this Part apply to all parts of the sea that are not included in the exclusive economic zone, in the territorial sea or in the internal waters of a State, or in the archipelagic waters of an archipelagic State. This article does not entail any abridgement of the freedoms enjoyed by all States in the exclusive economic zone in accordance with article 58.

ARTICLE 87

Freedom of the high seas

1. The high seas are open to all States, whether coastal or landlocked. Freedom of the high seas is exercised under the conditions laid down by this Convention and by other rules of international law. It comprises, *inter alia*, both for coastal and landlocked States:
   (a) freedom of navigation;
   (b) freedom of overflight;
   (c) freedom to lay submarine cables and pipelines, subject to Part VI;
   (d) freedom to construct artificial islands and other installations permitted under international law, subject to Part VI;
   (e) freedom of fishing, subject to the conditions laid down in section 2; and
   (f) freedom of scientific research, subject to Parts VI and XIII.
2. These freedoms shall be exercised by all States with due regard for the interests of other States in their exercise of the freedom of the high seas, and also with

due regard for the rights under this Convention with respect to activities in the Area.

ARTICLE 88

Reservation of the high seas for peaceful purposes

The high seas shall be reserved for peaceful purposes.

ARTICLE 89

Invalidity of claims of sovereignty over the high seas

No State may validly purport to subject any part of the high seas to its sovereignty.

ARTICLE 90

Right of navigation

Every State, whether coastal or landlocked, has the right to sail ships flying its flag on the high seas.

ARTICLE 91

Nationality of ships

1. Every State shall fix the conditions for the grant of its nationality to ships, for the registration of ships in its territory, and for the right to fly its flag. Ships have the nationality of the State whose flag they are entitled to fly. There must exist a genuine link between the State and the ship.
2. Every State shall issue, to ships, to which it has granted the right to fly its flag documents to that effect.

ARTICLE 92

Status of ships

1. Ships shall sail under the flag of one State only and, save in exceptional cases expressly provided for in international treaties or in this Convention, shall be subject to its exclusive jurisdiction on the high seas. A ship may not change its flag during a voyage or while in a port of call, save in the case of a real transfer of ownership or change of registry.
2. A ship which sails under the flags of two or more States, using them according to convenience, may not

claim any of the nationalities in question with respect to any other State, and may be assimilated to a ship without nationality.

ARTICLE 93

Ships flying the flag of the United Nations, its specialized agencies and the International Atomic Energy Agency

The preceding articles do not prejudice the question of ships employed on the official service of the United Nations, its specialized agencies or the International Atomic Energy Agency, flying the flag of the organization.

ARTICLE 94

Duties of the flag State

1. Every State shall effectively exercise its jurisdiction and control in administrative, technical and social matters over ships flying its flag.
2. In particular every State shall:
   (a) maintain a register of ships containing the names and particulars of ships flying its flag, except those which are excluded from generally accepted international regulations on account of their small size; and
   (b) assume jurisdiction under its internal law over each ship flying its flag and its master, officers and crew in respect of administrative, technical and social matters concerning the ship.
3. Every State shall take such measures for ships flying its flag as are necessary to ensure safety at sea with regard, *inter alia*, to —
   (a) the construction, equipment and seaworthiness of ships;
   (b) the manning of ships, the labour conditions and the training of crews, taking into account the applicable international instruments; and
   (c) the use of signals, the maintenance of communications and the prevention of collisions.
4. Such measures shall include those necessary to ensure:

(a) that each ship, before registration and thereafter, at appropriate intervals, is surveyed by a qualified surveyor of ships, and has on board such charts, nautical publications and navigational equipment and instruments as are appropriate for the safe navigation of the ship;

(b) that each ship is in the charge of a master and officers who possess appropriate qualifications, in particular, in seamanship, navigation, communications and marine engineering, and that the crew is appropriate in qualification and numbers for the type, size, machinery and equipment of the ship; and

(c) that the master, the officers and, to the extent appropriate, the crew are fully conversant with and required to observe the applicable international regulations concerning the safety of life at sea, the prevention of collisions, the prevention, reduction and control of marine pollution, and the maintenance of communications by radio.

5. In taking the measures called for in paragraphs 3 and 4, each State is required to conform to generally accepted international regulations, procedures and practices and to take any steps which may be necessary to secure their observance.

6. A State which has clear grounds to believe that proper jurisdiction and control with respect to a ship have not been exercised may report the facts to the flag State. Upon receiving such a report, the flag State shall investigate the matter and, if appropriate, take any action necessary to remedy the situation.

7. Each State shall cause an inquiry to be held by or before a suitably qualified person or persons into every marine casualty or incident of navigation on the high seas involving a ship flying its flag and causing loss of life or serious injury to nationals of another State or serious damage to ships or installations of another State or to the marine environment. The flag State and the other State shall cooperate in the conduct

of any inquiry held by that other State into any such marine casualty or incident of navigation.

ARTICLE 95

Immunity of warships on the high seas

Warships on the high seas have complete immunity from the jurisdiction of any State other than the flag State.

ARTICLE 96

Immunity of ships used only on government non-commercial service

Ships owned or operated by a State and used only on government non-commercial service shall, on the high seas, have complete immunity from the jurisdiction of any State other than the flag State.

ARTICLE 97

Penal jurisdiction in matters of collision or any other incident of navigation

1. In the event of a collision or any other incident of navigation concerning a ship on the high seas, involving the penal or disciplinary responsibility of the master or of any other person in the service of the ship, no penal or disciplinary proceedings may be instituted against such person except before the judicial or administrative authorities either of the flag State or of the State of which such person is a national.
2. In disciplinary matters, the State which has issued a master's certificate or a certificate of competence or a licence shall alone be competent, after due legal process, to pronounce the withdrawal of such certificates, even if the holder is not a national of the State which issued them.
3. No arrest or detention of the ship, even as a measure of investigation, shall be ordered by any authorities other than those of the flag State.

ARTICLE 98

Duty to render assistance

1. Every State shall require the master of a ship flying its

flag, in so far as he can do so without serious danger to the ship, the crew or the passengers:

(a) to render assistance to any person found at sea in danger of being lost;

(b) to proceed with all possible speed to the rescue of persons in distress, if informed of their need of assistance, in so far as such action may reasonably be expected of him; and

(c) after a collision, to render assistance to the other ship, its crew and its passengers and, where possible, to inform the other ship of the name of his own ship, its port of registry and the nearest port at which it will call.

2. Every coastal State shall promote the establishment, operation and maintenance of an adequate and effective search and rescue service regarding safety on and over the sea and, where circumstances so require, by way of mutual regional arrangements cooperate with neighbouring States for this purpose.

ARTICLE 99

Prohibition of the transport of slaves

Every State shall take effective measures to prevent and to punish the transport of slaves in ships authorized to fly its flag and to prevent the unlawful use of its flag for that purpose. Any slave taking refuge on board any ship, whatever its flag, shall ipso facto be free.

ARTICLE 100

Duty to cooperate in the repression of piracy

All States shall cooperate to the fullest possible extent in the repression of piracy on the high seas or in any other place outside the jurisdiction of any State.

ARTICLE 101

Definition of piracy

Piracy consists of any of the following acts:

(a) any illegal act of violence or detention, or any act of depredation, committed for private ends by the crew or the passengers of a private ship or a private aircraft, and directed:

(i) on the high seas, against another ship or aircraft, or against persons or property on board such ship or aircraft, or

(ii) against ship, aircraft, persons or property in a place outside the jurisdiction of any State;

(b) any act of voluntary participation in the operation of a ship or of an aircraft with knowledge of facts making it a pirate ship or aircraft; or

(c) any act of inciting or of intentionally facilitating an act described in subparagraph (a) or (b).

ARTICLE 102

Piracy by a warship, government ship or government aircraft whose crew has mutinied

The acts of piracy, as defined in article 101, committed by a warship, government ship or a government aircraft whose crew has mutinied and taken control of the ship or the aircraft are assimilated to acts committed by a private ship or aircraft.

ARTICLE 103

Definition of a pirate ship or aircraft

A ship or an aircraft is considered a pirate ship or aircraft if it is intended by the persons in dominant control to be used for the purpose of committing one of the acts referred to in article 101. The same applies if the ship or the aircraft has been used to commit any such act, so long as it remains under the control of the persons guilty of that act.

ARTICLE 104

Retention or loss of the nationality of a pirate ship or aircraft

A ship or an aircraft may retain its nationality although it has become a pirate ship or aircraft. The retention or loss of nationality is determined by the law of the State from which such nationality was derived.

ARTICLE 105

Seizure of a pirate ship or aircraft

On the high seas, or in any other place outside the jurisdiction of any State, every State may seize a pirate ship or aircraft, or a ship or an aircraft taken by piracy and under the control of pirates, and arrest the persons and seize the property on board. The courts of the State which carried out the seizure may decide upon the penalties to be imposed, and may also determine the action to be taken with regard to the ship, aircraft or property, subject to the rights of third parties acting in good faith.

ARTICLE 106

Liability for seizure without adequate grounds

Where the seizure of a ship or an aircraft on suspicion of piracy has been effected without adequate grounds, the State making the seizure shall be liable to the State, the nationality of which is possessed by the ship or an aircraft, for any loss or damage caused by the seizure.

ARTICLE 107

Ships and aircraft which are entitled to be seized on account of piracy

A seizure on account of piracy may be carried out only by warships or military aircraft, or other ships or aircraft clearly marked and identifiable as being on government service and authorized to that effect.

ARTICLE 108

Illicit traffic in narcotic drugs or psychotropic substances

1. All States shall cooperate in the suppression of illicit traffic in narcotic drugs and psychotropic substances engaged in by ships on the high seas contrary to international conventions.
2. Any State which has reasonable grounds for believing that a ship flying its flag is engaged in illicit traffic in narcotic drugs or psychotropic substances may request the cooperation of other States to suppress such traffic.

ARTICLE 109

Unauthorized broadcasting from the high seas

1. All States shall cooperate in the suppression of unauthorized broadcasting from the high seas.
2. For the purposes of this Convention, "unauthorized broadcasting" means the transmission of sound radio or television broadcasts from a ship or an installation on the high seas intended for reception by the general public contrary to international regulations, but excluding the transmission of distress calls.
3. Any person engaged in unauthorized broadcasting may be prosecuted before the court of —
   (a) the flag State of the ship;
   (b) the State of registry of the installation;
   (c) the State of which the person is a national;
   (d) any State where the transmissions can be received; or
   (e) any State where authorized radio communication is suffering interference.
4. On the high seas, a State having jurisdiction in accordance with paragraph 3, may, in conformity with article 110, arrest any person or ship engaged in unauthorized broadcasting and seize the broadcasting apparatus.

ARTICLE 110

Right of visit

1. Except where acts of interference derive from powers conferred by treaty, a warship which encounters on the high seas a foreign ship, other than a ship entitled to complete immunity in accordance with articles 95 and 96, is not justified in boarding it unless there is reasonable ground for suspecting that —
   (a) the ship is engaged in piracy;
   (b) the ship is engaged in the slave trade;
   (c) the ship is engaged in unauthorized broadcasting and the flag State of the warship has jurisdiction under article 109;

(d) the ship is without nationality; or

(e) though flying a foreign flag or refusing to show its flag, the ship is, in reality, of the same nationality as the warship.

2. In the cases provided for in paragraph 1, the warship may proceed to verify the ship's right to fly its flag. To this end, it may send a boat under the command of an officer to the suspected ship. If suspicion remains after the documents have been checked, it may proceed to a further examination on board the ship, which must be carried out with all possible consideration.

3. If the suspicions prove to be unfounded, and provided that the ship boarded has not committed any act justifying them, it shall be compensated for any loss or damage that may have been sustained.

4. These provisions apply *mutatis mutandis* to military aircraft.

5. These provisions also apply to any other duly authorized ships or aircraft clearly marked and identifiable as being on government service.

ARTICLE 111

Right of hot pursuit

1. The hot pursuit of a foreign ship may be undertaken when the competent authorities of the coastal State have good reason to believe that the ship has violated the laws and regulations of that State. Such pursuit must be commenced when the foreign ship or one of its boats is within the internal waters, the archipelagic waters, the territorial sea or the contiguous zone of the pursuing State, and may only be continued outside the territorial sea or the contiguous zone if the pursuit has not been interrupted. It is not necessary that, at the time when the foreign ship within the territorial sea or the contiguous zone receives the order to stop, the ship giving the order should likewise be within the territorial sea or the contiguous zone. If the foreign ship is within a contiguous zone, as defined in article 33, the pursuit may only be undertaken if there has

been a violation of the rights for the protection of which the zone was established.

2. The right of hot pursuit shall apply *mutatis mutandis* to violations in the exclusive economic zone or on the continental shelf, including the safety zones around the continental shelf installations, of the laws and regulations of the coastal State applicable, in accordance with this Convention, to the exclusive economic zone or the continental shelf, including such safety zones.
3. The right of hot pursuit ceases as soon as the ship pursued enters the territorial sea of its own State or of a third State.
4. Hot pursuit is not deemed to have begun unless the pursuing ship has satisfied itself by such practicable means as may be available that the ship pursued or one of its boats or other craft working as a team and using the ship pursued as a mother ship is within the limits of the territorial sea, or, as the case may be, within the contiguous zone or the exclusive economic zone or above the continental shelf. The pursuit may only be commenced after a visual or auditory signal to stop has been given at a distance which enables it to be seen or heard by the foreign ship.
5. The right of hot pursuit may be exercised only by warships or military aircraft, or other ships or aircraft clearly marked and identifiable as being on government service and authorized to that effect.
6. Where hot pursuit is effected by an aircraft:
   (a) the provisions of paragraphs 1 to 4 shall apply *mutatis mutandis*; and
   (b) the aircraft giving the order and to stop must itself actively pursue the ship until a ship or another aircraft of the coastal State, summoned by the aircraft, arrives to take over the pursuit, unless the aircraft is itself able to arrest the ship. It does not suffice to justify an arrest outside the territorial sea that the ship was merely sighted by the aircraft as an offender or suspected offender, if it was not both, ordered to stop and pursued by the aircraft

itself or other aircraft or ship which continue the pursuit without interruption.

7. The release of a ship arrested within the jurisdiction of a State and escorted to a port of that State for the purposes of an inquiry before the competent authorities may not be claimed solely on the ground that the ship, in the course of its voyage, was escorted across a portion of the exclusive economic zone or the high seas, if the circumstances rendered this necessary.
8. Where a ship has been stopped or arrested outside the territorial sea in circumstances which do not justify the exercise of the right of hot pursuit, it shall be compensated for any loss or damage that may have been thereby sustained.

ARTICLE 112

Right to lay submarine cables and pipelines

1. All States are entitled to lay submarine cables and pipelines on the bed of the high seas beyond the continental shelf.
2. Article 79, paragraph 5, applies to such cables and pipelines.

ARTICLE 113

Breaking or injury of a submarine cable or pipeline

Every State shall adopt the laws and regulations necessary to provide that the breaking or injury by a ship flying its flag or by a person subject to its jurisdiction of a submarine cable beneath the high seas done wilfully or through culpable negligence, in such a manner as to be liable to interrupt or obstruct telegraphic or telephonic communications, and similarly the breaking or injury of a submarine pipeline or high-voltage power cable, shall be a punishable offence. This provision shall apply also to conduct calculated or likely to result in such breaking or injury. However, it shall not apply to any break or injury caused by persons who acted merely with the legitimate object of saving their lives or their ships, after having taken all necessary precautions to avoid such break or injury.

ARTICLE 114

Breaking or injury by owners of a submarine cable or pipeline of another submarine cable or pipeline

Every State shall adopt the laws and regulations necessary to provide that, if persons subject to its jurisdiction who are the owners of a submarine cable or pipeline beneath the high seas, in laying or repairing that cable or pipeline, cause a break in or injury to another cable or pipeline, they shall bear the cost of the repairs.

ARTICLE 115

Indemnity for loss incurred in avoiding injury to a submarine cable or pipeline

Every State shall adopt the laws and regulations necessary to ensure that the owners of ships who can prove that they have sacrificed an anchor, a net or any other fishing gear, in order to avoid injuring a submarine cable or pipeline, shall be indemnified by the owner of the cable or pipeline, provided that the owner of the ship has taken all reasonable precautionary measures beforehand.

SECTION 2. CONSERVATION AND MANAGEMENT OF THE LIVING RESOURCES OF THE HIGH SEAS

ARTICLE 116

Right to fish on the high seas

All States have the right for their nationals to engage in fishing on the high seas subject to —

(a) their treaty obligations;

(b) the rights and duties as well as the interests of coastal States provided for, *inter alia,* in article 63, paragraph 2, and articles 64 to 67; and

(c) the provisions of this section.

ARTICLE 117

Duty of States to adopt with respect to their nationals measures for the conservation of the living resources of the high seas

All States have the duty to take, or to cooperate with other States in taking, such measures for their respective nationals as may be necessary for the conservation of the living resources of the high seas.

ARTICLE 118

Cooperation of States in the conservation and management of living resources

States shall cooperate with each other in the conservation and management of living resources in the areas of the high seas. States whose nationals exploit identical living resources, or different living resources in the same area, shall enter into negotiations with a view to taking the measures necessary for the conservation of the living resources concerned. They shall, as appropriate, cooperate to establish subregional or regional fisheries organizations to this end.

ARTICLE 119

Conservation of the living resources of the high seas

1. In determining the allowable catch and establishing other conservation measures for the living resources in the high seas, States shall:
   (a) take measures which are designed, on the best scientific evidence available to the States concerned, to maintain or to restore populations of harvested species at levels which can produce the maximum sustainable yield, as qualified by relevant environmental and economic factors, including the special requirements of developing States, and taking into account fishing patterns, the interdependence of stocks and any generally recommended international minimum standards, whether subregional, regional or global; and
   (b) take into consideration the effects on species associated with or dependent upon harvested species with a view to maintaining or restoring populations of such associated or dependent species above levels at which their reproduction may become seriously threatened.
2. Available scientific information, catch and fishing effort statistics, and other data relevant to the conservation

of fish stocks shall be contributed and exchanged on a regular basis through competent international organizations, whether subregional, regional or global, where appropriate and with participation by all States concerned.

3. States concerned shall ensure that conservation measures and their implementation do not discriminate in form or in fact against the fishermen of any State.

ARTICLE 120

Marine mammals

Article 65 also applies to the conservation and management of marine mammals in the high seas.

LAW OF SEA CONVENTION, 1982

PART-VIII

Regime of Islands

ARTICLE 121

Regime of islands

1. An island is a naturally formed area of land, surrounded by water, which is above water at high tide.
2. Except as provided for in paragraph 3, the territorial sea, the contiguous zone, the exclusive economic zone and the continental shelf of an island are determined in accordance with the provisions of this Convention applicable to other land territory.
3. Rocks which cannot sustain human habitation or economic life of their own shall have no exclusive economic zone or continental shelf.

LAW OF SEA CONVENTION, 1982

PART-IX

Enclosed or Semi-Enclosed Seas

ARTICLE 122

Definition

For the purposes of this Convention, "enclosed or semi-enclosed sea" means a gulf, basin or sea surrounded by two or more States and connected to another sea or the ocean by a narrow outlet or consisting entirely or primarily of the territorial seas and the exclusive economic zones of two or more coastal States.

ARTICLE 123

Cooperation of States bordering enclosed or semi-enclosed seas

States bordering an enclosed or a semi-enclosed sea should cooperate with each other in the exercise of their rights and in the performance of their duties under this Convention. To this end they shall endeavour, directly or through an appropriate regional organization:

(a) to coordinate the management, conservation, exploration and exploitation of the living resources of the sea;

(b) to coordinate the implementation of their rights and duties with respect to the protection and preservation of the marine environment;

(c) to coordinate their scientific research policies and undertake, where appropriate, joint programmes of scientific research in the area;

(d) to invite, as appropriate, other interested States or international organizations to cooperate with them in furtherance of the provisions of this article.

LAW OF SEA CONVENTION, 1982

PART-X

Right of Access of Landlocked States to and from the Sea and Freedom of Transit

ARTICLE 124

Use of terms

1. For the purposes of this Convention:
   (a) "landlocked State" means a State which has no sea-coast;
   (b) "transit State" means a State, with or without a sea-coast, situated between a landlocked State and the sea, through whose territory traffic in transit passes;
   (c) "traffic in transit" means transit of persons, baggage, goods and means of transport across the territory of one or more transit States, when the passage across such territory, with or without trans-shipment, warehousing, breaking bulk or change in the mode of transport, is only a portion of a complete journey which begins or terminates within the territory of the landlocked State; and
   (d) "means of transport" means:
      (i) railway rolling-stock, sea, lake and river craft and road vehicles;
      (ii) where local conditions so require, porters and pack animals.
2. Landlocked States and transit States may, by agreement between them, include as means of transport pipelines and gas lines and means of transport other than those included in paragraph 1.

ARTICLE 125

Right of access to and from the sea and freedom of transit

1. Landlocked States shall have the right of access to and from the sea for the purpose of exercising the rights provided for in this Convention, including those relating to the freedom of the high seas and the common heritage of mankind. To this end, landlocked States shall enjoy freedom of transit through the territory of transit States by all means of transport.
2. The terms and modalities for exercising freedom of transit shall be agreed between the landlocked States and transit States concerned through bilateral, subregional or regional agreements.
3. Transit States, in the exercise of their full sovereignty over their territory, shall have the right to take all measures necessary to ensure that the rights and facilities, provided for in this Part, for landlocked States shall in no way infringe their legitimate interests.

ARTICLE 126

Exclusion of application of the most-favoured-nation clause

The provisions of this Convention, as well as special agreements relating to the exercise of the right of access to and from the sea, establishing rights and facilities on account of the special geographical position of landlocked States, are excluded from the application of the most-favoured-nation clause.

ARTICLE 127

Customs duties, taxes and other charges

1. Traffic in transit shall not be subject to any customs duties, taxes or other charges except charges levied for specific services rendered in connection with such traffic.
2. Means of transport in transit and other facilities provided for and used by landlocked States shall not be subject to taxes or charges higher than those levied for the use of means of transport of the transit State.

ARTICLE 128

Free zones and other customs facilities

For the convenience of traffic in transit, free zones or other customs facilities may be provided at the ports of entry and exit in the transit States, by agreement between those States and the landlocked States.

ARTICLE 129

Cooperation in the construction and improvement of means of transport

Where there are no means of transport in transit States to give effect to the freedom of transit or where the existing means, including the port installations and equipment, are inadequate in any respect, the transit States and landlocked States concerned may cooperate in constructing or improving them.

ARTICLE 130

Measures to avoid or eliminate delays or other difficulties of a technical nature in traffic in transit

1. Transit States shall take all appropriate measures to avoid delays or other difficulties of a technical nature in traffic in transit.
2. Should such delays or difficulties occur, the competent authorities of the transit States and landlocked States concerned shall cooperate towards their expeditious elimination.

ARTICLE 131

Equal treatment in maritime ports

Ships flying the flag of landlocked States shall enjoy treatment equal to that accorded to other foreign ships in maritime ports.

ARTICLE 132

Grant of greater transit facilities

This Convention does not entail in anyway the withdrawal of transit facilities which are greater than those provided for in this Convention and which are agreed between States Parties to this Convention or granted by a State Party. This Convention also does not preclude such grant of greater facilities in the future.

LAW OF SEA CONVENTION, 1982

PART-XI

The Area

SECTION 1. GENERAL PROVISIONS

ARTICLE 133

Use of terms

For the purposes of this Part:

(a) "resources" means all solid, liquid or gaseous mineral resources *in situ* in the Area at or beneath the seabed, including polymetallic nodules; and

(b) resources, when recovered from the Area, are referred to as "minerals".

ARTICLE 134

Scope of this Part

1. This Part applies to the Area.
2. Activities in the Area shall be governed by the provisions of this Part.
3. The requirements concerning deposit of, and publicity to be given to, the charts or lists of geographical coordinates showing the limits referred to in article 1, paragraph 1(1), are set forth in Part VI.
4. Nothing in this article affects the establishment of the outer limits of the continental shelf in accordance with Part VI or the validity of agreements relating to delimitation between States with opposite or adjacent coasts.

ARTICLE 135

Legal status of the superjacent waters and air space

Neither this Part nor any rights granted or exercised pursuant thereto shall affect the legal status of the waters superjacent to the Area or that of the air space above those waters.

SECTION 2. PRINCIPLES GOVERNING THE AREA

ARTICLE 136

Common heritage of mankind

The Area and its resources are the common heritage of mankind.

ARTICLE 137

Legal status of the Area and its resources

1. No State shall claim or exercise sovereignty or sovereign rights over any part of the Area or its resources, nor shall any State or natural or juridical person appropriate any part thereof. No such claim or exercise of sovereignty or sovereign rights nor such appropriation shall be recognized.
2. All rights in the resources of the Area are vested in mankind as a whole, on whose behalf the Authority shall act. These resources are not subject to alienation. The minerals recovered from the Area, however, may only be alienated in accordance with this Part and the rules, regulations and procedures of the Authority.
3. No State or natural or juridical person shall claim, acquire or exercise rights with respect to the minerals recovered from the Area except in accordance with this Part. Otherwise, no such claim, acquisition or exercise of such rights shall be recognized.

ARTICLE 138

General conduct of States in relation to the Area

The general conduct of States in relation to the Area shall be in accordance with the provisions of this Part, the principles embodied in the Charter of the United Nations and other rules of international law in the interests of maintaining peace and security, and promoting international cooperation and mutual understanding.

ARTICLE 139

Responsibility to ensure compliance and liability for damage

1. States Parties shall have the responsibility to ensure that activities in the Area, whether carried out by States

Parties, or state enterprises, or natural or juridical persons who possess the nationality of States Parties or are effectively controlled by them or their nationals, shall be carried out in conformity with this Part. The same responsibility applies to international organizations for activities in the Area carried out by such organizations.

2. Without prejudice to the rules of international law and Annex III, article 22, damage caused by the failure of a State Party or an international organization to carry out its responsibilities under this Part shall entail liability; States Parties or international organizations acting together shall bear joint and several liability. A State Party shall not, however, be liable for damage caused by any failure to comply with this Part by a person whom it has sponsored under article 153, paragraph 2(b), if the State Party has taken all necessary and appropriate measures to secure effective compliance under article 153, paragraph 4, and Annex III, article 4, paragraph 4.
3. States Parties that are members of international organizations shall take appropriate measures to ensure the implementation of this article with respect to such organizations.

ARTICLE 140

Benefit of mankind

1. Activities in the Area shall, as specifically provided for in this Part, be carried out for the benefit of mankind as a whole, irrespective of the geographical location of States, whether coastal or landlocked, and taking into particular consideration the interests and needs of developing States and of peoples who have not attained full independence, or other self-governing status recognized by the United Nations in accordance with General Assembly resolution 1514 (XV) and other relevant General Assembly resolutions.
2. The Authority shall provide for the equitable sharing of financial and other economic benefits derived from activities in the Area through any appropriate

mechanism, on a non-discriminatory basis, in accordance with article 160, paragraph 2(f)(i).

ARTICLE 141

Use of the Area exclusively for peaceful purposes

The Area shall be open to use exclusively for peaceful purposes by all States, whether coastal or landlocked, without discrimination and without prejudice to the other provisions of this Part.

ARTICLE 142

Rights and legitimate interests of coastal States

1. Activities in the Area, with respect to resource deposits in the Area which lie across limits of national jurisdiction, shall be conducted with due regard to the rights and legitimate interests of any coastal State across whose jurisdiction such deposits lie.
2. Consultations, including a system of prior notification, shall be maintained with the State concerned, with a view to avoiding infringement of such rights and interests. In cases where activities in the Area may result in the exploitation of resources lying within national jurisdiction, the prior consent of the coastal State concerned shall be required.
3. Neither this Part nor any rights granted or exercised pursuant thereto shall affect the rights of coastal States to take such measures consistent with the relevant provisions of Part XII, as may be necessary, to prevent, mitigate or eliminate grave and imminent danger to their coastline, or related interests from pollution or threat thereof or from other hazardous occurrences resulting from or caused by any activities in the Area.

ARTICLE 143

Marine scientific research

1. Marine scientific research in the Area shall be carried out exclusively for peaceful purposes and for the benefit of mankind as a whole, in accordance with Part XIII.
2. The Authority may carry out marine scientific research concerning the Area and its resources, and may enter

into contracts for that purpose. The Authority shall promote and encourage the conduct of marine scientific research in the Area, and shall coordinate and disseminate the results of such research and analysis when available.

3. States Parties may carry out marine scientific research in the Area. States Parties shall promote international cooperation in marine scientific research in the Area by:

(a) participating in international programmes and encouraging cooperation in marine scientific research by personnel of different countries and of the Authority;

(b) ensuring that programmes are developed through the Authority or other international organizations, as appropriate, for the benefit of developing States and technologically less developed States with a view to —

(i) strengthening their research capabilities,

(ii) training their personnel and the personnel of the Authority in the techniques and applications of research, and

(iii) fostering the employment of their qualified personnel in research in the Area;

(c) effectively disseminating the results of research and analysis when available, through the Authority or other international channels when appropriate.

ARTICLE 144

Transfer of technology

1. The Authority shall take measures in accordance with this Convention:

(a) to acquire technology and scientific knowledge relating to activities in the Area; and

(b) to promote and encourage the transfer to developing States of such technology and scientific knowledge so that all States Parties benefit therefrom.

2. To this end, the Authority and States Parties shall cooperate in promoting the transfer of technology and scientific knowledge relating to activities in the Area so that the Enterprise and all States Parties may benefit therefrom. In particular, they shall initiate and promote:
   (a) programmes for the transfer of technology to the Enterprise and to the developing States with regard to activities in the Area, including, *inter alia*, facilitating the access of the Enterprise and of the developing States to the relevant technology, under fair and reasonable terms and conditions; and
   (b) measures directed towards the advancement of the technology of the Enterprise and the domestic technology of the developing States, particularly by providing opportunities to personnel from the Enterprise and from the developing States for training in marine science and technology and for their full participation in activities in the Area.

ARTICLE 145

Protection of the marine environment

Necessary measures shall be taken, in accordance with this Convention, with respect to activities in the Area to ensure effective protection for the marine environment from harmful effects which may arise from such activities. To this end the Authority shall adopt appropriate rules, regulations and procedures for *inter alia*:

(a) the prevention, reduction and control of pollution and other hazards to the marine environment, including the coastline, and of interference with the ecological balance of the marine environment, particular attention being paid to the need for protection from harmful effects of such activities as drilling, dredging, excavation, disposal of waste, construction and operation or maintenance of installations, pipelines and other devices related to such activities; and

(b) the protection and conservation of the natural resources of the Area and the prevention of damage to the flora and fauna of the marine environment.

ARTICLE 146

Protection of human life

With respect to activities in the Area, necessary measures shall be taken to ensure effective protection of human life. To this end the Authority shall adopt appropriate rules, regulations and procedures to supplement existing international law as embodied in relevant treaties.

ARTICLE 147

Accommodation of activities in the Area and in the marine environment

1. Activities in the Area shall be carried out with reasonable regard for other activities in the marine environment.
2. Installations used for carrying out activities in the Area shall be subject to the following conditions:
   (a) such installations shall be erected, emplaced and removed solely in accordance with this Part and subject to the rules, regulations and procedures of the Authority. Due notice must be given of the erection, emplacement and removal of such installations, and permanent means for giving warning of their presence must be maintained;
   (b) such installations may not be established where interference may be caused to the use of recognized sea lanes essential to international navigation or in areas of intense fishing activity;
   (c) safety zones shall be established around such installations with appropriate markings to ensure the safety of both navigation and the installations. The configuration and location of such safety zones shall not be such as to form a belt impeding the lawful access of shipping to particular maritime zones or navigation along international sea lanes;
   (d) such installations shall be used exclusively for peaceful purposes;
   (e) such installations do not possess the status of islands. They have no territorial sea of their own, and their presence does not affect the delimitation

of the territorial sea, the exclusive economic zone or the continental shelf.

3. Other activities in the marine environment shall be conducted with reasonable regard for activities in the Area.

ARTICLE 148

Participation of developing States in activities in the Area

The effective participation of developing States in activities in the Area shall be promoted, as specifically provided for in this Part, having due regard to their special interests and needs, and, in particular, to the special need of the landlocked and geographically disadvantaged among them to overcome obstacles arising from their disadvantaged location, including remoteness from the Area and difficulty of access to and from it.

ARTICLE 149

Archaeological and historical objects

All objects of an archaeological and historical nature found in the Area shall be preserved or disposed of for the benefit of mankind as a whole, particular regard being paid to the preferential rights of the State or country of origin, or the State of cultural origin, or the State of historical and archaeological origin.

SECTION 3. DEVELOPMENT OF RESOURCES OF THE AREA

ARTICLE 150

Policies relating to activities in the Area

Activities in the Area shall, as specifically provided for in this Part, be carried out in such a manner as to foster healthy development of the world economy and balanced growth of international trade, and to promote international cooperation for the overall development of all countries, especially developing States, and with a view to ensuring:

(a) the development of the resources of the Area;

(b) orderly, safe and rational management of the resources of the Area, including the efficient conduct of activities in the Area and, in accordance with sound principles of conservation, the avoidance of unnecessary waste;

(c) the expansion of opportunities for participation in such activities consistent in particular with articles 144 and 148;

(d) participation in revenues by the Authority and the transfer of technology to the Enterprise and developing States as provided for in this Convention;

(e) increased availability of the minerals derived from the Area as needed in conjunction with minerals derived from other sources, to ensure supplies to consumers of such minerals;

(f) the promotion of just and stable prices remunerative to producers and fair to consumers for minerals derived both from the Area and from other sources, and the promotion of long-term equilibrium between supply and demand;

(g) the enhancement of opportunities for all States Parties, irrespective of their social and economic systems or geographical location, to participate in the development of the resources of the Area and the prevention of monopolization of activities in the Area;

(h) the protection of developing countries from adverse effects on their economies or on their export earnings resulting from a reduction in the price of an affected mineral, or in the volume of exports of that mineral, to the extent that such reduction is caused by activities in the Area, as provided in article 151;

(i) the development of the common heritage for the benefit of mankind as a whole; and

(j) conditions of access to markets for the imports of minerals produced from the resources of the Area and for imports of commodities produced from such minerals shall not be more favourable than the most favourable applied to imports from other sources.

ARTICLE 151

Production policies

1. (a) Without prejudice to the objectives set forth in article 150 and for the purpose of implementing subparagraph (h) of that article, the Authority, acting through existing forums or such new arrangements, or agreements, as may be appropriate, in which all interested parties, including both producers and consumers, participate, shall take measures necessary to promote the growth, efficiency and stability of markets for those commodities produced from the minerals derived from the Area, at prices remunerative to producers and fair to consumers. All States Parties shall cooperate to this end.

   (b) The Authority shall have the right to participate in any commodity conference dealing with those commodities and in which all interested parties including both producers and consumers participate. The Authority shall have the right to become a party to any arrangement or agreement resulting from such conferences. Participation of the Authority in any organs established under those arrangements or agreements shall be in respect of production in the Area and in accordance with the relevant rules of those organs.

   (c) The Authority shall carry out its obligations under the arrangements or agreements referred to in this paragraph in a manner which assures a uniform and non-discriminatory implementation in respect of all production in the Area of the minerals concerned. In doing so, the Authority shall act in a manner consistent with the terms of existing contracts and approved plans of work of the Enterprise.

2. (a) During the interim period, specified in paragraph 3, commercial production shall not be undertaken pursuant to an approved plan of work until the operator has applied for and has been issued a

production authorization by the Authority. Such production authorizations may not be applied for or issued more than five years prior to the planned commencement of commercial production under the plan of work unless, having regard to the nature and timing of project development, the rules, regulations and procedures of the Authority prescribe another period.

(b) In the application for the production authorization, the operator shall specify the annual quantity of nickel expected to be recovered under the approved plan of work. The application shall include a schedule of expenditures to be made by the operator after he has received the authorization which are reasonably calculated to allow him to begin commercial production on the date planned.

(c) For the purposes of subparagraphs (a) and (b), the Authority shall establish appropriate performance requirements in accordance with Annex III, article 17.

(d) The Authority shall issue a production authorization for the level of production applied for unless the sum of that level and the levels already authorized exceeds the nickel production ceiling, as calculated pursuant to paragraph 4, in the year of issuance of the authorization, during any year of planned production falling within the interim period.

(e) When issued, the production authorization and approved application shall become a part of the approved plan of work.

(f) If the operator's application for a production authorization is denied, pursuant to subparagraph (d), the operator may apply again to the Authority at any time.

3. The interim period shall begin five years prior to 1st January of the year in which the earliest commercial production is planned to commence under an approved plan of work. If the earliest commercial production is delayed beyond the year originally planned, the

beginning of the interim period and the production ceiling originally calculated shall be adjusted accordingly. The interim period shall last 25 years or until the end of the Review Conference referred to in article 155 or until the day when such new arrangements or agreements as are referred to in paragraph 1 enter into force, whichever is earliest. The Authority shall resume the power provided in this article for the remainder of the interim period if the said arrangements or agreements should lapse or become ineffective for any reason whatsoever.

4. (a) The production ceiling for any year of the interim period shall be the sum of —

   (i) the difference between the trend line values for nickel consumption, as calculated pursuant to subparagraph (b), for the year immediately prior to the year of the earliest commercial production and the year immediately prior to the commencement of the interim period; and

   (ii) sixty per cent of the difference between the trend line values for nickel consumption, as calculated pursuant to subparagraph (b), for the year for which the production authorization is being applied for and the year immediately prior to the year of the earliest commercial production.

   (b) For the purposes of subparagraph (a):

   (i) trend line values used for computing the nickel production ceiling shall be those annual nickel consumption values on a trend line computed during the year in which a production authorization is issued. The trend line shall be derived from a linear regression of the logarithms of actual nickel consumption for the most recent 15-year period for which such data are available, time being the independent variable. This trend line shall be referred to as the original trend line;

(ii) if the annual rate of increase of the original trend line is less than 3 per cent, then the trend line used to determine the quantities referred to in subparagraph (a) shall instead be one passing through the original trend line at the value for the first year of the relevant 15-year period, and increasing at 3 per cent annually; provided however that the production ceiling established for any year of the interim period may not in any case exceed the difference between the original trend line value for that year and the original trend line value for the year immediately prior to the commencement of the interim period.

5. The Authority shall reserve to the Enterprise for its initial production a quantity of 38,000 metric tonnes of nickel from the available production ceiling calculated pursuant to paragraph 4.

6. (a) An operator may in any year produce less than or up to 8 per cent more than the level of annual production of minerals from polymetallic nodules specified in his production authorization, provided that the overall amount of production shall not exceed that specified in the authorization. Any excess over 8 per cent and up to 20 per cent in any year, or any excess in the first and subsequent years following two consecutive years in which excesses occur, shall be negotiated with the Authority, which may require the operator to obtain a supplementary production authorization to cover additional production.

(b) Applications for such supplementary production authorizations shall be considered by the Authority only after all pending applications by operators who have not yet received production authorizations have been acted upon and due account has been taken of other likely applicants. The Authority shall be guided by the principle of not exceeding the total production allowed under the production ceiling in any year of the interim period. It shall not authorize the production, under any plan of work, of a quantity in excess of 46,500 metric tonnes of nickel per year.

7. The levels of production of other metals such as copper, cobalt and manganese extracted from the polymetallic nodules that are recovered pursuant to a production authorization should not be higher than those which would have been produced had the operator produced the maximum level of nickel from those nodules pursuant to this article. The Authority shall establish rules, regulations and procedures pursuant to Annex III, article 17, to implement this paragraph.

8. Rights and obligations relating to unfair economic practices under relevant multilateral trade agreements shall apply to the exploration for and to the exploitation of minerals from the Area. In the settlement of disputes arising under this provision, States Parties which are Parties to such multilateral trade agreements shall have recourse to the dispute settlement procedures of such agreements.

9. The Authority shall have the power to limit the level of production of minerals from the Area, other than minerals from polymetallic nodules, under such conditions and applying such methods as may be appropriate by adopting regulations in accordance with article 161, paragraph 8.

10. Upon the recommendation of the Council on the basis of advice from the Economic Planning Commission, the Assembly shall establish a system of compensation or take other measures of economic adjustment assistance including cooperation with specialized agencies and other international organizations to assist developing countries which suffer serious adverse effects on their export earnings or economies resulting from a reduction in the price of an affected mineral or in the volume of exports of that mineral, to the extent that such reduction is caused by activities in the Area. The Authority on request shall initiate studies on the problems

of those States which are likely to be most seriously affected with a view to minimizing their difficulties and assisting them in their economic adjustment.

ARTICLE 152

Exercise of powers and functions by the Authority

1. The Authority shall avoid discrimination in the exercise of its powers and functions, including the granting of opportunities for activities in the Area.
2. Nevertheless, special consideration for developing States, including particular consideration for the landlocked and geographically disadvantaged among them, specifically provided for in this Part shall be permitted.

ARTICLE 153

System of exploration and exploitation

1. Activities in the Area shall be organized, carried out and controlled by the Authority on behalf of mankind as a whole, in accordance with this article as well as other relevant provisions of this Part and the relevant Annexes, and the rules, regulations and procedures of the Authority.
2. Activities in the Area shall be carried out as prescribed in paragraph 3:
   (a) by the Enterprise, and
   (b) in association with the Authority by States Parties, or state enterprises or natural or juridical persons which possess the nationality of States Parties or are effectively controlled by them or their nationals, when sponsored by such States, or any group of the foregoing which meets the requirements provided in this Part and in Annex III.
3. Activities in the Area shall be carried out in accordance with a formal written plan of work drawn up in accordance with Annex III and approved by the Council after review by the Legal and Technical Commission. In the case of activities in the Area carried out as authorized by the Authority by the entities specified in paragraph 2(b), the plan of work shall, in accordance

with Annex III, article 3, be in the form of a contract. Such contracts may provide for joint arrangements in accordance with Annex III, article 11.

4. The Authority shall exercise such control over activities in the Area as is necessary for the purpose of securing compliance with the relevant provisions of this Part and the Annexes relating thereto, and the rules, regulations and procedures of the Authority, and the plans of work approved in accordance with paragraph 3. States Parties shall assist the Authority by taking all measures necessary to ensure such compliance in accordance with article 139.
5. The Authority shall have the right to take, at any time, any measures provided for under this Part to ensure compliance with its provisions and the exercise of the functions of control and regulation assigned to it thereunder or under any contract. The Authority shall have the right to inspect all installations in the Area used in connection with activities in the Area.
6. A contract under paragraph 3 shall provide for security of tenure. Accordingly, the contract shall not be revised, suspended or terminated except in accordance with Annex III, articles 18 and 19.

ARTICLE 154

Periodic review

Every five years from the entry into force of this Convention, the Assembly shall undertake a general and systematic review of the manner in which the international regime of the Area established in this Convention has operated in practice. In the light of this review, the Assembly may take, or recommend that other organs take, measures in accordance with the provisions and procedures of this Part and the Annexes relating thereto, which will lead to the improvement of the operation of the regime.

ARTICLE 155

The Review Conference

1. Fifteen years from 1st January of the year in which the earliest commercial production commences under an

approved plan of work, the Assembly shall convene a conference for the review of those provisions of this Part and the relevant Annexes which govern the system of exploration and exploitation of the resources of the Area. The Review Conference shall consider in detail, in the light of the experience acquired during that period:

(a) whether the provisions of this Part which govern the system of exploration and exploitation of the resources of the Area have achieved their aims in all respects, including whether they have benefited mankind as a whole;

(b) whether, during the 15-year period, reserved areas have been exploited in an effective and balanced manner in comparison with non-reserved areas;

(c) whether the development and use of the Area and its resources have been undertaken in such a manner as to foster healthy development of the world economy and balanced growth of international trade;

(d) whether monopolization of activities in the Area has been prevented;

(e) whether the policies set forth in articles 150 and 151 have been fulfilled; and

(f) whether the system has resulted in the equitable sharing of benefits derived from activities in the Area, taking into particular consideration the interests and needs of the developing States.

2. The Review Conference shall ensure the maintenance of the principle of the common heritage of mankind, the international regime designed to ensure equitable exploitation of the resources of the Area for the benefit of all countries, especially the developing States, and an Authority to organize, conduct and control activities in the Area. It shall also ensure the maintenance of the principles laid down in this Part with regard to the exclusion of claims or exercise of sovereignty over any part of the Area, the rights of States and their general conduct in relation to the Area, and their participation

in activities in the Area in conformity with this Convention, the prevention of monopolization of activities in the Area, the use of the Area exclusively for peaceful purposes, economic aspects of activities in the Area, marine scientific research, transfer of technology, protection of the marine environment, protection of human life, rights of coastal States, the legal status of the waters superjacent to the Area and that of the air space above those waters and accommodation between activities in the Area and other activities in the marine environment.

3. The decision-making procedure applicable at the Review Conference shall be the same as that applicable at the Third United Nations Conference on the Law of the Sea. The Conference shall make every effort to reach agreement on any amendments by way of consensus and there should be no voting on such matters until all efforts at achieving consensus have been exhausted.
4. If, five years after its commencement, the Review Conference has not reached agreement on the system of exploration and exploitation of the resources of the Area, it may decide during the ensuing 12 months, by a three-fourths majority of the States Parties, to adopt and submit to the States Parties for ratification or accession such amendments changing or modifying the system as it determines necessary and appropriate. Such amendments shall enter into force for all States Parties 12 months after the deposit of instruments of ratification or accession by three-fourths of the States Parties.
5. Amendments adopted by the Review Conference pursuant to this article shall not affect rights acquired under existing contracts.

SECTION 4. THE AUTHORITY

Sub-section A. *General Provisions*

ARTICLE 156

Establishment of the Authority

1. There is hereby established the International Seabed

Authority which shall function in accordance with this Part.

2. All States Parties are *ipso facto* members of the Authority.
3. Observers at the Third United Nations Conference on the Law of the Sea who have signed the Final Act and who are not referred to in article 305, paragraph 1(c), (d), (e) or (f), shall have the right to participate in the Authority as observers, in accordance with its rules, regulations and procedures.
4. The seat of the Authority shall be in Jamaica.
5. The Authority may establish such regional centres or offices as it deems necessary for the exercise of its functions.

ARTICLE 157

Nature and fundamental principles of the Authority

1. The Authority is the organization through which States Parties shall, in accordance with this Part, organize and control activities in the Area, particularly with a view to administering the resources of the Area.
2. The powers and functions of the Authority shall be those expressly conferred upon it by this Convention. The Authority shall have such incidental powers, consistent with this Convention, as are implicit in and necessary for the exercise of those powers and functions with respect to activities in the Area.
3. The Authority is based on the principle of the sovereign equality of all its members.
4. All members of the Authority shall fulfil in good faith the obligations assumed by them, in accordance with this Part, in order to ensure to all of them the rights and benefits resulting from membership.

ARTICLE 158

Organs of the Authority

1. There are hereby established, as the principal organs of the Authority, an Assembly, a Council and a Secretariat.
2. There is hereby established the Enterprise, the organ

through which the Authority shall carry out the functions referred to in article 170, paragraph 1.

3. Such subsidiary organs as may be found necessary may be established in accordance with this Part.
4. Each principal organ of the Authority and the Enterprise shall be responsible for exercising those powers and functions which are conferred upon it. In exercising such powers and functions, each organ shall avoid taking any action which may derogate from or impede the exercise of specific powers and functions conferred upon another organ.

Sub-section B. *The Assembly*

ARTICLE 159

Composition, procedure and voting

1. The Assembly shall consist of all the members of the Authority. Each member shall have one representative in the Assembly, who may be accompanied by alternates and advisers.
2. The Assembly shall meet in regular annual sessions and in such special sessions as may be decided by the Assembly, or convened by the Secretary-General at the request of the Council or of a majority of the members of the Authority.
3. Sessions shall take place at the seat of the Authority unless otherwise decided by the Assembly.
4. The Assembly shall adopt its rules of procedure. At the beginning of each regular session, it shall elect its President and such other officers as may be required. They shall hold office until a new President and other officers are elected at the next regular session.
5. A majority of the members of the Assembly shall constitute a quorum.
6. Each member of the Assembly shall have one vote.
7. Decisions on questions of procedure, including decisions to convene special sessions of the Assembly, shall be taken by a majority of the members present and voting.

8. Decisions on questions of substance shall be taken by a two-thirds majority of the members present and voting, provided that such majority includes a majority of the members participating in the session. When the issue arises as to whether a question is one of substance or not, that question shall be treated as one of substance unless otherwise decided by the Assembly by the majority required for decisions on questions of substance.
9. When a question of substance comes up for voting for the first time, the President may, and shall, if requested by at least one-fifth of the members of the Assembly, defer the issue of taking a vote on that question for a period not exceeding five calendar days. This rule may be applied only once to any question, and shall not be applied so as to defer the question beyond the end of the session.
10. Upon a written request addressed to the President and sponsored by, at least, one-fourth of the members of the Authority for an advisory opinion on the conformity with this Convention of a proposal before the Assembly on any matter, the Assembly shall request the Seabed Disputes Chamber of the International Tribunal for the Law of the Sea to give an advisory opinion thereon and shall defer voting on that proposal pending receipt of the advisory opinion by the Chamber. If the advisory opinion is not received before the final week of the session in which it is requested, the Assembly shall decide when it will meet to vote upon the deferred proposal.

ARTICLE 160

Powers and functions

1. The Assembly, as the sole organ of the Authority consisting of all the members, shall be considered the supreme organ of the Authority to which the other principal organs shall be accountable as specifically provided for in this Convention. The Assembly shall have the power to establish general policies in conformity with the relevant provisions of this

Convention on any question or matter within the competence of the Authority.

2. In addition, the powers and functions of the Assembly shall be:

(a) to elect the members of the Council in accordance with article 161;

(b) to elect the Secretary-General from among the candidates proposed by the Council;

(c) to elect, upon the recommendation of the Council, the members of the Governing Board of the Enterprise and the Director-General of the Enterprise;

(d) to establish such subsidiary organs as it finds necessary for the exercise of its functions, in accordance with this Part. In the composition of these subsidiary organs due account shall be taken of the principle of equitable geographical distribution and of special interests and the need for members qualified and competent in the relevant technical questions dealt with by such organs;

(e) to assess the contributions of members to the administrative budget of the Authority in accordance with an agreed scale of assessment based upon the scale used for the regular budget of the United Nations until the Authority shall have sufficient income from other sources to meet its administrative expenses;

(f) (i) to consider and approve, upon the recommendation of the Council, the rules, regulations and procedures on the equitable sharing of financial and other economic benefits derived from activities in the Area and the payments and contributions made pursuant to article 82, taking into particular consideration the interests and needs of developing States and peoples who have not attained full independence or other self-governing status. If the Assembly does not approve the recommendations of the Council, the Assembly shall return them to the Council for reconsideration in the light of the views expressed by the Assembly, and

(ii) to consider and approve the rules, regulations and procedures of the Authority, and any amendments thereto, provisionally adopted by the Council pursuant to article 162, paragraph 2(o)(ii). These rules, regulations and procedures shall relate to prospecting, exploration and exploitation in the Area, the financial management and internal administration of the Authority, and, upon the recommendation of the Governing Board of the Enterprise, to the transfer of funds from the Enterprise to the Authority;

(g) to decide upon the equitable sharing of financial and other economic benefits derived from activities in the Area, consistent with this Convention and the rules, regulations and procedures of the Authority;

(h) to consider and approve the proposed annual budget of the Authority submitted by the Council;

(i) to examine periodic reports from the Council and from the Enterprise and special reports requested from the Council or any other organ of the Authority;

(j) to initiate studies and make recommendations for the purpose of promoting international cooperation concerning activities in the Area and encouraging the progressive development of international law relating thereto and its codification;

(k) to consider problems of a general nature in connection with activities in the Area arising in particular for developing States, as well as those problems for States in connection with activities in the Area that are due to their geographical location, particularly for landlocked and geographically disadvantaged States;

(l) to establish, upon the recommendation of the Council, on the basis of advice from the Economic

Planning Commission, a system of compensation or other measures of economic adjustment assistance as provided in article 151, paragraph 10;

(m) to suspend the exercise of rights and privileges of membership pursuant to article 185; and

(n) to discuss any question or matter within the competence of the Authority and to decide as to which organ of the Authority shall deal with any such question or matter not specifically entrusted to a particular organ, consistent with the distribution of powers and functions among the organs of the Authority.

Sub-section C. *The Council*

ARTICLE 161

Composition, procedure and voting

1. The Council shall consist of 36 members of the Authority elected by the Assembly in the following order:

(a) four members from among those States Parties which, during the last five years for which statistics are available, have either consumed more than 2 per cent of total world consumption or have had net imports of more than 2 per cent of total world imports of the commodities produced from the categories of minerals to be derived from the Area, and in any case one State from the Eastern European (Socialist) region, as well as the largest consumer;

(b) four members from among the eight States Parties which have the largest investments in preparation for and in the conduct of activities in the Area, either directly or through their nationals, including at least one State from the Eastern European (Socialist) region;

(c) four members from among States Parties which on the basis of production in areas under their jurisdiction are major net exporters of the categories of minerals to be derived from the Area, including at least two developing States whose exports of such minerals have a substantial bearing upon their economies;

(d) six members from among developing States Parties, representing special interests. The special interests to be represented shall include those of States with large populations, States which are land-locked or geographically disadvantaged, States which are major importers of the categories of minerals to be derived from the Area, States which are potential producers of such minerals, and least developed States;

(e) eighteen members elected according to the principle of ensuring an equitable geographical distribution of seats in the Council as a whole, provided that each geographical region shall have at least one member elected under this subparagraph. For this purpose, the geographical regions shall be Africa, Asia, Eastern European (Socialist), Latin America and Western European and Others.

2. In electing the members of the Council, in accordance with paragraph 1, the Assembly shall ensure that:

(a) landlocked and geographically disadvantaged States are represented to a degree which is reasonably proportionate to their representation in the Assembly;

(b) coastal States, especially developing States, which do not qualify under paragraph 1(a), (b), (c) or (d) are represented to a degree which is reasonably proportionate to their representation in the Assembly; and

(c) each group of States Parties to be represented on the Council is represented by those members, if any, which are nominated by that group.

3. Elections shall take place at regular sessions of the Assembly. Each member of the Council shall be elected for four years. At the first election, however, the term

of one half of the members of each group referred to in paragraph 1 shall be two years.

4. Members of the Council shall be eligible for re-election, but due regard should be paid to the desirability of rotation of membership.
5. The Council shall function at the seat of the Authority, and shall meet as often as the business of the Authority may require, but not less than three times a year.
6. A majority of the members of the Council shall constitute a quorum.
7. Each member of the Council shall have one vote.
8. (a) Decisions on questions of procedure shall be taken by a majority of the members present and voting.

   (b) Decisions on questions of substance arising under the following provisions shall be taken by a two-thirds majority of the members present and voting, provided that such majority includes a majority of the members of the Council: article 162, paragraph 2, subparagraphs (f); (g); (h); (i); (n); (p); (v); article 191.

   (c) Decisions on questions of substance arising under the following provisions shall be taken by a three-fourths majority of the members present and voting, provided that such majority includes a majority of the members of the Council: article 162, paragraph 1; article 162, paragraph 2, subparagraphs (a); (b); (c); (d); (e); (l); (q); (r); (s); (t); (u) in cases of non-compliance by a contractor or a sponsor; (w) provided that orders issued thereunder may be binding for not more than 30 days unless confirmed by a decision taken in accordance with subparagraph (d); article 162, paragraph 2, subparagraphs (x); (y); (z); article 163, paragraph 2; article 174, paragraph 3; Annex IV, article 11.

   (d) Decisions on questions of substance arising under the following provisions shall be taken by consensus: article 162, paragraph 2(m) and (o); adoption of amendments to Part XI.

(e) For the purposes of subparagraphs (d), (f) and (g), "consensus" means the absence of any formal objection. Within 14 days of the submission of a proposal to the Council, the President of the Council shall determine whether there would be a formal objection to the adoption of the proposal. If the President determines that there would be such an objection, the President shall establish and convene, within three days following such determination, a conciliation committee consisting of not more than nine members of the Council, with the President as chairman, for the purpose of reconciling the differences and producing a proposal which can be adopted by consensus. The committee shall work expeditiously and report to the Council within 14 days following its establishment. If the committee is unable to recommend a proposal which can be adopted by consensus, it shall set out in its report the grounds on which the proposal is being opposed.

(f) Decisions on questions not listed above which the Council is authorized to take by the rules, regulations and procedures of the Authority or otherwise shall be taken pursuant to the subparagraphs of this paragraph specified in the rules, regulations and procedures or, if not specified therein, then pursuant to the subparagraph determined by the Council if possible in advance, by consensus.

(g) When the issue arises as to whether a question is within subparagraph (a), (b), (c) or (d), the question shall be treated as being within the subparagraph requiring the higher or highest majority or consensus as the case may be, unless otherwise decided by the Council by the said majority or by consensus.

9. The Council shall establish a procedure whereby a member of the Authority not represented on the Council may send a representative to attend a meeting of the Council when a request is made by such member, or a matter particularly affecting it is under consideration.

Such a representative shall be entitled to participate in the deliberations but not to vote.

ARTICLE 162

Powers and functions

1. The Council is the executive organ of the Authority. The Council shall have the power to establish, in conformity with this Convention and the general policies established by the Assembly, the specific policies to be pursued by the Authority on any question or matter within the competence of the Authority.
2. In addition, the Council shall:
   (a) supervise and coordinate the implementation of the provisions of this Part on all questions and matters within the competence of the Authority and invite the attention of the Assembly to cases of non-compliance;
   (b) propose to the Assembly a list of candidates for the election of the Secretary-General;
   (c) recommend to the Assembly candidates for the election of the members of the Governing Board of the Enterprise and the Director-General of the Enterprise;
   (d) establish, as appropriate, and with due regard to economy and efficiency, such subsidiary organs as it finds necessary for the exercise of its functions, in accordance with this Part. In the composition of subsidiary organs, emphasis shall be placed on the need for members qualified and competent in relevant technical matters dealt with by those organs provided that due account shall be taken of the principle of equitable geographical distribution and of special interests;
   (e) adopt its rules of procedure including the method of selecting its president;
   (f) enter into agreements with the United Nations or other international organizations on behalf of the Authority and within its competence, subject to approval by the Assembly;

(g) consider the reports of the Enterprise and transmit them to the Assembly with its recommendations;

(h) present to the Assembly annual reports and such special reports as the Assembly may request;

(i) issue directives to the Enterprise in accordance with article 170;

(j) approve plans of work in accordance with Annex III, article 6. The Council shall act upon each plan of work within 60 days of its submission by the Legal and Technical Commission at a session of the Council in accordance with the following procedures:

 (i) if the Commission recommends the approval of a plan of work, it shall be deemed to have been approved by the Council if no member of the Council submits in writing to the President within 14 days a specific objection alleging non-compliance with the requirements of Annex III, article 6. If there is an objection, the conciliation procedure set forth in article 161, paragraph 8(e), shall apply. If, at the end of the conciliation procedure, the objection is still maintained, the plan of work shall be deemed to have been approved by the Council unless the Council disapproves it by consensus among its members excluding any State or States making the application or sponsoring the applicant;

 (ii) if the Commission recommends the disapproval of a plan of work or does not make a recommendation, the Council may approve the plan of work by a three-fourths majority of the members present and voting, provided that such majority includes a majority of the members participating in the session;

(k) approve plans of work submitted by the Enterprise in accordance with Annex IV, article 12, applying, *mutatis mutandis,* the procedures set forth in subparagraph (j);

(l) exercise control over activities in the Area in accordance with article 153, paragraph 4, and the rules, regulations and procedures of the Authority;

(m) take, upon the recommendation of the Economic Planning Commission, necessary and appropriate measures in accordance with article 150, subparagraph (h), to provide protection from the adverse economic effects specified therein;

(n) make recommendations to the Assembly, on the basis of advice from the Economic Planning Commission, for a system of compensation or other measures of economic adjustment assistance as provided in article 151, paragraph 10;

(o) (i) recommend to the Assembly rules, regulations and procedures on the equitable sharing of financial and other economic benefits derived from activities in the Area and the payments and contributions made pursuant to article 82, taking into particular consideration the interests and needs of the developing States and peoples who have not attained full independence or other self-governing status;

(ii) adopt and apply provisionally, pending approval by the Assembly, the rules, regulations and procedures of the Authority, and any amendments thereto, taking into account the recommendations of the Legal and Technical Commission or other subordinate organ concerned. These rules, regulations and procedures shall relate to prospecting, exploration and exploitation in the Area, and the financial management and internal administration of the Authority. Priority shall be given to the adoption of rules, regulations and procedures for the exploration for and exploitation of polymetallic nodules. Rules, regulations and procedures for the exploration for and exploitation of any resource other than polymetallic nodules shall be adopted within three years from the date of a request to the Authority by any of its members to adopt such rules, regulations and procedures in respect of such resource. All rules, regulations and procedures shall remain in effect on a provisional basis, until approved by the Assembly or until amended by the Council in the light of any views expressed by the Assembly;

(p) review the collection of all payments to be made by or to the Authority in connection with operations pursuant to this Part;

(q) make the selection from among applicants for production authorizations pursuant to Annex III, article 7, where such selection is required by that provision;

(r) submit the proposed annual budget of the Authority to the Assembly for its approval;

(s) make recommendations to the Assembly concerning policies on any question or matter within the competence of the Authority;

(t) make recommendations to the Assembly concerning suspension of the exercise of the rights and privileges of membership pursuant to article 185;

(u) institute proceedings on behalf of the Authority before the Seabed Disputes Chamber in cases of non-compliance;

(v) notify the Assembly upon a decision by the Seabed Disputes Chamber in proceedings instituted under subparagraph (u), and make any recommendations which it may find appropriate with respect to measures to be taken;

(w) issue emergency orders, which may include orders for the suspension or adjustment of operations, to prevent serious harm to the marine environment arising out of activities in the Area;

(x) disapprove areas for exploitation by contractors or the Enterprise in cases where substantial evidence indicates the risk of serious harm to the marine environment;

(y) establish a subsidiary organ for the elaboration of draft financial rules, regulations and procedures relating to —

  (i) financial management in accordance with articles 171 to 175; and

  (ii) financial arrangements in accordance with Annex III, article 13 and article 17, paragraph 1(c);

(z) establish appropriate mechanisms for directing and supervising a staff of inspectors who shall inspect activities in the Area to determine whether this Part, the rules, regulations and procedures of the Authority, and the terms and conditions of any contract with the Authority are being complied with.

ARTICLE 163

Organs of the Council

1. There are hereby established the following organs of the Council:

   (a) an Economic Planning Commission; and

   (b) a Legal and Technical Commission.

2. Each Commission shall be composed of 15 members, elected by the Council from among the candidates nominated by the States Parties. However, if necessary, the Council may decide to increase the size of either Commission having due regard to economy and efficiency.

3. Members of a Commission shall have appropriate qualifications in the area of competence of that Commission. States Parties shall nominate candidates of the highest standards of competence and integrity with qualifications in relevant fields so as to ensure the effective exercise of the functions of the Commissions.

4. In the election of members of the Commissions, due account shall be taken of the need for equitable geographical distribution and the representation of special interests.
5. No State Party may nominate more than one candidate for the same Commission. No person shall be elected to serve on more than one Commission.
6. Members of the Commissions shall hold office for a term of five years. They shall be eligible for re-election for a further term.
7. In the event of the death, incapacity or resignation of a member of a Commission prior to the expiration of the term of office, the Council shall elect for the remainder of the term, a member from the same geographical region or area of interest.
8. Members of Commissions shall have no financial interest in any activity relating to exploration and exploitation in the Area. Subject to their responsibilities to the Commissions upon which they serve, they shall not disclose, even after the termination of their functions, any industrial secret, proprietary data which are transferred to the Authority in accordance with Annex III, article 14, or any other confidential information coming to their knowledge by reason of their duties for the Authority.
9. Each Commission shall exercise its functions in accordance with such guidelines and directives as the Council may adopt.
10. Each Commission shall formulate and submit to the Council for approval such rules and regulations as may be necessary for the efficient conduct of the Commission's functions.
11. The decision-making procedures of the Commissions shall be established by the rules, regulations and procedures of the Authority. Recommendations to the Council shall, where necessary, be accompanied by a summary on the divergencies of opinion in the Commission.

12. Each Commission shall normally function at the seat of the Authority and shall meet as often as is required for the efficient exercise of its functions.
13. In the exercise of its functions, each Commission may, where appropriate, consult another commission, any competent organ of the United Nations or of its specialized agencies or any international organizations with competence in the subject-matter of such consultation.

ARTICLE 164

The Economic Planning Commission

1. Members of the Economic Planning Commission shall have appropriate qualifications such as those relevant to mining, management of mineral resource activities, international trade or international economics. The Council shall endeavour to ensure that the membership of the Commission reflects all appropriate qualifications. The Commission shall include at least two members from developing States whose exports of the categories of minerals to be derived from the Area have a substantial bearing upon their economies.
2. The Commission shall:
   (a) propose, upon the request of the Council, measures to implement decisions relating to activities in the Area taken in accordance with this Convention;
   (b) review the trends of and the factors affecting supply, demand and prices of minerals which may be derived from the Area, bearing in mind the interests of both importing and exporting countries, and in particular, of the developing States among them;
   (c) examine any situation likely to lead to the adverse effects referred to in article 150, subparagraph (h), brought to its attention by the State Party or States Parties concerned, and make appropriate recommendations to the Council; and
   (d) propose to the Council for submission to the Assembly, as provided in article 151, paragraph 10, a system of compensation or other measures

of economic adjustment assistance for developing States which suffer adverse effects caused by activities in the Area. The Commission shall make the recommendations to the Council that are necessary for the application of the system or other measures adopted by the Assembly in specific cases.

ARTICLE 165

The Legal and Technical Commission

1. Members of the Legal and Technical Commission shall have appropriate qualifications such as those relevant to exploration for, and exploitation and processing of mineral resources, oceanology, protection of the marine environment, or economic or legal matters relating to ocean mining and related fields of expertise. The Council shall endeavour to ensure that the membership of the Commission reflects all appropriate qualifications.
2. The Commission shall:
   (a) make recommendations with regard to the exercise of the Authority's functions upon the request of the Council;

   (b) review formal written plans of work for activities in the Area in accordance with article 153, paragraph 3, and submit appropriate recommendations to the Council. The Commission shall base its recommendations solely on the grounds stated in Annex III and shall report fully thereon to the Council;

   (c) supervise, upon the request of the Council, activities in the Area, where appropriate, in consultation and collaboration with any entity carrying out such activities or State or States concerned and report to the Council;

   (d) prepare assessments of the environmental implications of activities in the Area;

   (e) make recommendations to the Council on the protection of the marine environment, taking into account the views of recognized experts in that field;

(f) formulate and submit to the Council the rules, regulations and procedures referred to in article 162, paragraph 2(o), taking into account all relevant factors including assessments of the environmental implications of activities in the Area;

(g) keep such rules, regulations and procedures under review and recommend to the Council from time to time such amendments thereto as it may deem necessary or desirable;

(h) make recommendations to the Council regarding the establishment of a monitoring programme to observe, measure, evaluate and analyse, by recognized scientific methods, on a regular basis, the risks or effects of pollution of the marine environment resulting from activities in the Area, ensure that existing regulations are adequate and are complied with and coordinate the implementation of the monitoring programme approved by the Council;

(i) recommend to the Council that proceedings be instituted on behalf of the Authority before the Seabed Disputes Chamber, in accordance with this Part and the relevant Annexes taking into account particularly article 187;

(j) make recommendations to the Council with respect to measures to be taken, upon a decision by the Seabed Disputes Chamber in proceedings instituted in accordance with subparagraph (i);

(k) make recommendations to the Council to issue emergency orders, which may include orders for the suspension or adjustment of operations, to prevent serious harm to the marine environment arising out of activities in the Area. Such recommendations shall be taken up by the Council on a priority basis;

(l) make recommendations to the Council to disapprove areas for exploitation by contractors or the Enterprise in cases where substantial evidence indicates the risk of serious harm to the marine environment;

(m) make recommendations to the Council regarding the direction and supervision of a staff of inspectors who shall inspect activities in the Area to determine whether the provisions of this Part, the rules, regulations and procedures of the Authority, and the terms and conditions of any contract with the Authority are being complied with; and

(n) calculate the production ceiling and issue production authorizations on behalf of the Authority pursuant to article 151, paragraphs 2 to 7, following any necessary selection among applicants for production authorizations by the Council in accordance with Annex III, article 7.

3. The members of the Commission shall, upon request by any State Party or other party concerned, be accompanied by a representative of such State or other party concerned when carrying out their function of supervision and inspection.

Sub-section D. *The Secretariat*

ARTICLE 166

The Secretariat

1. The Secretariat of the Authority shall comprise a Secretary-General and such staff as the Authority may require.
2. The Secretary-General shall be elected for four years by the Assembly from among the candidates proposed by the Council and may be re-elected.
3. The Secretary-General shall be the chief administrative officer of the Authority, and shall act in that capacity in all meetings of the Assembly, of the Council and of any subsidiary organ, and shall perform such other administrative functions as are entrusted to the Secretary-General by these organs.
4. The Secretary-General shall make an annual report to the Assembly on the work of the Authority.

ARTICLE 167

The staff of the Authority

1. The staff of the Authority shall consist of such qualified scientific and technical and other personnel as may be required to fulfil the administrative functions of the Authority.
2. The paramount consideration in the recruitment and employment of the staff and in the determination of their conditions of service shall be the necessity of securing the highest standards of efficiency, competence and integrity. Subject to this consideration, due regard shall be paid to the importance of recruiting the staff on as wide a geographical basis as possible.
3. The staff shall be appointed by the Secretary-General. The terms and conditions on which they shall be appointed, remunerated and dismissed shall be in accordance with the rules, regulations and procedures of the Authority.

ARTICLE 168

International character of the Secretariat

1. In the performance of their duties the Secretary-General and the staff shall not seek or receive instructions from any government or from any other source external to the Authority. They shall refrain from any action which might reflect on their position as international officials responsible only to the Authority. Each State Party undertakes to respect the exclusively international character of the responsibilities of the Secretary-General and the staff and not to seek to influence them in the discharge of their responsibilities. Any violation of responsibilities by a staff member shall be submitted to the appropriate administrative tribunal as provided in the rules, regulations and procedures of the Authority.
2. The Secretary-General and the staff shall have no financial interest in any activity relating to exploration and exploitation in the Area. Subject to their responsibilities to the Authority, they shall not disclose, even after the termination of their functions, any

industrial secret, proprietary data which are transferred to the Authority in accordance with Annex III, article 14, or any other confidential information coming to their knowledge by reason of their employment with the Authority.

3. Violations of the obligations of a staff member of the Authority, set forth in paragraph 2, shall, on the request of a State Party affected by such violation, or a natural or juridical person, sponsored by a State Party as provided in article 153, paragraph 2(b), and affected by such violation, be submitted by the Authority against the staff member concerned to a tribunal designated by the rules, regulations and procedures of the Authority. The Party affected shall have the right to take part in the proceedings. If the tribunal so recommends, the Secretary-General shall dismiss the staff member concerned.
4. The rules, regulations and procedures of the Authority shall contain such provisions as are necessary to implement this article.

ARTICLE 169

Consultation and cooperation with international and non-governmental organizations

1. The Secretary-General shall, on matters within the competence of the Authority, make suitable arrangements, with the approval of the Council, for consultation and cooperation with international and non-governmental organizations recognized by the Economic and Social Council of the United Nations.
2. Any organization with which the Secretary-General has entered into an arrangement, under paragraph 1, may designate representatives to attend meetings of the organs of the Authority as observers, in accordance with the rules of procedure of these organs. Procedures shall be established for obtaining the views of such organizations in appropriate cases.
3. The Secretary-General may distribute to States Parties written reports submitted by the non-governmental

organizations, referred to in paragraph 1, on subjects in which they have special competence and which are related to the work of the Authority.

Sub-section E. *The Enterprise*

ARTICLE 170

The Enterprise

1. The Enterprise shall be the organ of the Authority which shall carry out activities in the Area directly, pursuant to article 153, paragraph 2(a), as well as the transporting, processing and marketing of minerals recovered from the Area.
2. The Enterprise shall, within the framework of the international legal personality of the Authority, have such legal capacity as is provided for in the Statute set forth in Annex IV. The Enterprise shall act in accordance with this Convention and the rules, regulations and procedures of the Authority, as well as the general policies established by the Assembly, and shall be subject to the directives and control of the Council.
3. The Enterprise shall have its principal place of business at the seat of the Authority.
4. The Enterprise shall, in accordance with article 173, paragraph 2, and Annex IV, article 11, be provided with such funds as it may require to carry out its functions, and shall receive technology as provided in article 144 and other relevant provisions of this Convention.

Sub-section F. *Financial Arrangements of the Authority*

ARTICLE 171

Funds of the Authority

The funds of the Authority shall include:

(a) assessed contributions made by members of the Authority in accordance with article 160, paragraph 2(e);

(b) funds received by the Authority pursuant to Annex III, article 13, in connection with activities in the Area;

(c) funds transferred from the Enterprise in accordance with Annex IV, article 10;

(d) funds borrowed pursuant to article 174;

(e) voluntary contributions made by members or other entities; and

(f) payments to a compensation fund, in accordance with article 151, paragraph 10, whose sources are to be recommended by the Economic Planning Commission.

ARTICLE 172

Annual budget of the Authority

The Secretary-General shall draft the proposed annual budget of the Authority and submit it to the Council. The Council shall consider the proposed annual budget and submit it to the Assembly, together with any recommendations thereon. The Assembly shall consider and approve the proposed annual budget in accordance with article 160, paragraph 2(h).

ARTICLE 173

Expenses of the Authority

1. The contributions referred to in article 171, subparagraph (a), shall be paid into a special account to meet the administrative expenses of the Authority until the Authority has sufficient funds from other sources to meet those expenses.

2. The administrative expenses of the Authority shall be a first call upon the funds of the Authority. Except for the assessed contributions referred to in article 171, subparagraph (a), the funds which remain after payment of administrative expenses may, *inter alia*:

   (a) be shared in accordance with article 140 and article 160, paragraph 2(g);

   (b) be used to provide the Enterprise with funds in accordance with article 170, paragraph 4; and

   (c) be used to compensate developing States in accordance with article 151, paragraph 10, and article 160, paragraph 2.

ARTICLE 174

Borrowing power of the Authority

1. The Authority shall have the power to borrow funds.
2. The Assembly shall prescribe the limits on the borrowing power of the Authority in the financial regulations adopted pursuant to article 160, paragraph 2.
3. The Council shall exercise the borrowing power of the Authority.
4. States Parties shall not be liable for the debts of the Authority.

ARTICLE 175

Annual audit

The records, books and accounts of the Authority, including its annual financial statements, shall be audited annually by an independent auditor appointed by the Assembly.

Sub-section G. *Legal Status, Privileges and Immunities*

ARTICLE 176

Legal status

The Authority shall have international legal personality and such legal capacity as may be necessary for the exercise of its functions and the fulfilment of its purposes.

ARTICLE 177

Privileges and immunities

To enable the Authority to exercise its functions, it shall enjoy in the territory of each State Party the privileges and immunities set forth in this sub-section. The privileges and immunities relating to the Enterprise shall be those set forth in Annex IV, article 13.

ARTICLE 178

Immunity from legal process

The Authority, its property and assets, shall enjoy immunity from legal process except to the extent that the Authority expressly waives this immunity in a particular case.

ARTICLE 179

Immunity from search and any form of seizure

The property and assets of the Authority, wherever located and by whomsoever held, shall be immune from search, requisition, confiscation, expropriation or any other form of seizure by executive or legislative action.

ARTICLE 180

Exemption from restrictions, regulations, controls and moratoria

The property and assets of the Authority shall be exempt from restrictions, regulations, controls and moratoria of any nature.

ARTICLE 181

Archives and official communications of the Authority

1. The archives of the Authority, wherever located, shall be inviolable.
2. Proprietary data, industrial secrets or similar information and personnel records shall not be placed in archives which are open to public inspection.
3. With regard to its official communications, the Authority shall be accorded by each State Party treatment no less favourable than that accorded by that State to other international organizations.

ARTICLE 182

Privileges and immunities of certain persons connected with the Authority

Representatives of States Parties attending meetings of the Assembly, the Council or organs of the Assembly or the Council, and the Secretary-General and staff of the Authority, shall enjoy in the territory of each State Party:

(a) immunity from legal process with respect to acts performed by them in the exercise of their functions, except to the extent that the State which they represent or the Authority, as appropriate, expressly waives this immunity in a particular case; and

(b) if they are not nationals of that State Party, the same exemptions from immigration restrictions, alien registration requirements and national service obligations, the same facilities as regards exchange restrictions and the same treatment in respect of travelling facilities as are accorded by that State to the representatives, officials and employees of comparable rank of other States Parties.

ARTICLE 183

Exemption from taxes and customs duties

1. Within the scope of its official activities, the Authority, its assets and property, its income, and its operations and transactions, authorized by this Convention, shall be exempt from all direct taxation and goods imported or exported for its official use shall be exempt from all customs duties. The Authority shall not claim exemption from taxes which are no more than charges for services rendered.
2. When purchases of goods or services of substantial value necessary for the official activities of the Authority are made by or on behalf of the Authority, and when the price of such goods or services includes taxes or duties, appropriate measures shall, to the extent practicable, be taken by States Parties to grant exemption, from such taxes or duties or provide for their reimbursement. Goods imported or purchased under an exemption provided for in this article, shall not be sold or otherwise disposed of in the territory of the State Party which granted the exemption, except under conditions agreed with that State Party.
3. No tax shall be levied by States Parties on or in respect of salaries and emoluments paid or any other form of payment made by the Authority to the Secretary-General and staff of the Authority, as well as experts performing missions for the Authority, who are not their nationals.

Sub-section H. *Suspension of the Exercise of Rights and Privileges of Members*

ARTICLE 184

Suspension of the exercise of voting rights

A State Party which is in arrears in the payment of its financial contributions to the Authority shall have no vote if the amount of its arrears equals or exceeds the amount of the contributions due from it for the preceding two full years. The Assembly may, nevertheless, permit such a member to vote if it is satisfied that the failure to pay is due to conditions beyond the control of the member.

ARTICLE 185

Suspension of exercise of rights and privileges of membership

1. A State Party which has grossly and persistently violated the provisions of this Part may be suspended from the exercise of the rights and privileges of membership by the Assembly upon the recommendation of the Council.
2. No action may be taken under paragraph 1 until the Seabed Disputes Chamber has found that a State Party has grossly and persistently violated the provisions of this Part.

SECTION 5. SETTLEMENT OF DISPUTES AND ADVISORY OPINIONS

ARTICLE 186

Seabed Disputes Chamber of the International Tribunal for the Law of the Sea

The establishment of the Seabed Disputes Chamber and the manner in which it shall exercise its jurisdiction shall be governed by the provisions of this section, of Part XV and of Annex VI.

ARTICLE 187

Jurisdiction of the Seabed Disputes Chamber

The Seabed Disputes Chamber shall have jurisdiction under this Part and the Annexes relating thereto in disputes with respect to activities in the Area falling within the following categories:

(a) disputes between States Parties concerning the interpretation or application of this Part and the Annexes relating thereto;

(b) disputes between a State Party and the Authority concerning:

  (i) acts or omissions of the Authority or of a State Party alleged to be in violation of this Part or the Annexes relating thereto or of rules, regulations and procedures of the Authority adopted in accordance therewith; or

  (ii) acts of the Authority alleged to be in excess of jurisdiction or a misuse of power;

(c) disputes between parties to a contract, being States Parties, the Authority or the Enterprise, the state enterprises and the natural or juridical persons referred to in article 153, paragraph 2(b), concerning:

  (i) the interpretation or application of a relevant contract or a plan of work; or

  (ii) acts or omissions of a party to the contract relating to activities in the Area and directed to the other party or directly affecting its legitimate interests;

(d) disputes between the Authority and a prospective contractor who has been sponsored by a State as provided in article 153, paragraph 2(b), and has duly fulfilled the conditions referred to in Annex III, article 4, paragraph 6, and article 13, paragraph 2, concerning the refusal of a contract or a legal issue arising in the negotiation of the contract;

(e) disputes between the Authority and a State Party, a state enterprise or a natural or juridical person sponsored by a State Party as provided for in article 153, paragraph 2(b), where it is alleged that the Authority has incurred liability as provided in Annex III, article 22; and

(f) any other disputes for which the jurisdiction of the Chamber is specifically provided in this Convention.

ARTICLE 188

Submission of disputes to a special chamber of the International Tribunal for the Law of the Sea or an *ad hoc* chamber of the Seabed Disputes Chamber or to binding commercial arbitration

1. Disputes between States Parties referred to in article 187, subparagraph (a), may be submitted:
   (a) at the request of the parties to the dispute, to a special chamber of the International Tribunal for the Law of the Sea to be formed in accordance with Annex VI, articles 15 and 17; or
   (b) at the request of any party to the dispute, to an *ad hoc* chamber of the Seabed Disputes Chamber to be formed in accordance with Annex VI, article 36.
2. (a) Disputes concerning the interpretation or application of a contract referred to in article 187, subparagraph (c)(i), shall be submitted, at the request of any party to the dispute, to binding commercial arbitration, unless the parties otherwise agree. A commercial arbitral tribunal to which the dispute is submitted shall have no jurisdiction to decide any question of interpretation of this Convention. When the dispute also involves a question of the interpretation of Part XI and the Annexes relating thereto, with respect to activities in the Area, that question shall be referred to the Seabed Disputes Chamber for a ruling.
   (b) If, at the commencement of or in the course of such arbitration, the arbitral tribunal determines, either at the request of any party to the dispute or *proprio motu*, that its decision depends upon a ruling of the Seabed Disputes Chamber, the arbitral tribunal shall refer such question to the Seabed Disputes Chamber for such ruling. The arbitral tribunal shall then proceed to render its award in conformity with the ruling of the Seabed Disputes Chamber.

(c) In the absence of a provision in the contract on the arbitration procedure to be applied in the dispute, the arbitration shall be conducted in accordance with the UNCITRAL Arbitration Rules or such other arbitration rules as may be prescribed in the rules, regulations and procedures of the Authority, unless the parties to the dispute otherwise agree.

ARTICLE 189

Limitation on jurisdiction with regard to decisions of the Authority

The Seabed Disputes Chamber shall have no jurisdiction with regard to the exercise by the Authority of its discretionary powers, in accordance with this Part; in no case shall it substitute its discretion for that of the Authority. Without prejudice to article 191, in exercising its jurisdiction pursuant to article 187, the Seabed Disputes Chamber shall not pronounce itself on the question of whether any rules, regulations and procedures of the Authority are in conformity with this Convention, nor declare invalid any such rules, regulations and procedures. Its jurisdiction, in this regard, shall be confined to deciding claims that the application of any rules, regulations and procedures of the Authority in individual cases would be in conflict with the contractual obligations of the parties to the dispute or their obligations under this Convention, claims concerning excess of jurisdiction or misuse of power, and to claims for damages to be paid or other remedy to be given to the party concerned for the failure of the other party to comply with its contractual obligations or its obligations under this Convention.

ARTICLE 190

Participation and appearance of sponsoring States Parties in proceedings

1. If a natural or juridical person is a party to a dispute referred to in article 187, the sponsoring State shall be given notice thereof and shall have the right to participate in the proceedings by submitting written or oral statements.

2. If an action is brought against a State Party by a natural or juridical person sponsored by another State Party in a dispute referred to in article 187, subparagraph (c), the respondent State may request the State sponsoring that person to appear in the proceedings on behalf of that person. Failing such appearance, the respondent State may arrange to be represented by a juridical person of its nationality.

ARTICLE 191

Advisory opinions

The Seabed Disputes Chamber shall give advisory opinions at the request of the Assembly or the Council on legal questions arising within the scope of their activities. Such opinions shall be given as a matter of urgency.

LAW OF SEA CONVENTION, 1982

PART-XII

Protection and Preservation of the Marine Environment

SECTION 1. GENERAL PROVISIONS

ARTICLE 192

General obligation

States have the obligation to protect and preserve the marine environment.

ARTICLE 193

Sovereign right of States to exploit their natural resources

States have the sovereign right to exploit their natural resources pursuant to their environmental policies and in accordance with their duty to protect and preserve the marine environment.

ARTICLE 194

Measures to prevent, reduce and control pollution of the marine environment

1. States shall take, individually or jointly as appropriate, all measures consistent with this Convention that are necessary to prevent, reduce and control pollution of the marine environment from any source, using for this purpose the best practicable means at their disposal and in accordance with their capabilities, and they shall endeavour to harmonize their policies in this connection.
2. States shall take all measures necessary to ensure that activities under their jurisdiction or control are so conducted as not to cause damage by pollution to other States and their environment, and that pollution arising from incidents or activities under their jurisdiction or control does not spread beyond the areas where

they exercise sovereign rights in accordance with this Convention.

3. The measures taken, pursuant to this Part, shall deal with all sources of pollution of the marine environment. These measures shall include, *inter alia*, those designed to minimize to the fullest possible extent:
   (a) the release of toxic, harmful or noxious substances, especially those which are persistent, from land-based sources, from or through the atmosphere or by dumping;
   (b) pollution from vessels, in particular measures for preventing accidents and dealing with emergencies, ensuring the safety of operations at sea, preventing intentional and unintentional discharges, and regulating the design, construction, equipment, operation and manning of vessels;
   (c) pollution from installations and devices used in exploration or exploitation of the natural resources of the seabed and subsoil, in particular measures for preventing accidents and dealing with emergencies, ensuring the safety of operations at sea, and regulating the design, construction, equipment, operation and manning of such installations or devices; and
   (d) pollution from other installations and devices operating in the marine environment, in particular measures for preventing accidents and dealing with emergencies, ensuring the safety of operations at sea, and regulating the design, construction, equipment, operation and manning of such installations or devices.
4. In taking measures to prevent, reduce or control pollution of the marine environment, States shall refrain from unjustifiable interference with activities carried out by other States in the exercise of their rights and in pursuance of their duties in conformity with this Convention.
5. The measures taken, in accordance with this Part, shall include those necessary to protect and preserve rare or

fragile ecosystems as well as the habitat of depleted, threatened or endangered species and other forms of marine life.

ARTICLE 195

Duty not to transfer damage or hazards or transform one type of pollution into another

In taking measures to prevent, reduce and control pollution of the marine environment, States shall act so as not to transfer, directly or indirectly, damage or hazards from one area to another or transform one type of pollution into another.

ARTICLE 196

Use of technologies or introduction of alien or new species

1. States shall take all measures necessary to prevent, reduce and control pollution of the marine environment resulting from the use of technologies under their jurisdiction or control, or the intentional or accidental introduction of species, alien or new, to a particular part of the marine environment, which may cause significant and harmful changes thereto.
2. This article does not affect the application of this Convention regarding the prevention, reduction and control of pollution of the marine environment.

SECTION 2. GLOBAL AND REGIONAL COOPERATION

ARTICLE 197

Cooperation on a global or regional basis

States shall cooperate on a global basis and, as appropriate, on a regional basis, directly or through competent international organizations, in formulating and elaborating international rules, standards and recommended practices and procedures consistent with this Convention, for the protection and preservation of the marine environment, taking into account characteristic regional features.

ARTICLE 198

Notification of imminent or actual damage

When a State becomes aware of cases in which the marine

environment is in imminent danger of being damaged or has been damaged by pollution, it shall immediately notify other States it deems likely to be affected by such damage, as well as the competent international organizations.

ARTICLE 199

Contingency plans against pollution

In the cases referred to in article 198, States in the area affected, in accordance with their capabilities, and the competent international organizations shall cooperate, to the extent possible, in eliminating the effects of pollution and preventing or minimizing the damage. To this end, States shall jointly develop and promote contingency plans for responding to pollution incidents in the marine environment.

ARTICLE 200

Studies, research programmes and exchange of information and data

States shall cooperate, directly or through competent international organizations, for the purpose of promoting studies, undertaking programmes of scientific research and encouraging the exchange of information and data acquired about pollution of the marine environment. They shall endeavour to participate actively in regional and global programmes to acquire knowledge for the assessment of the nature and extent of pollution, exposure to it, and its pathways, risks and remedies.

ARTICLE 201

Scientific criteria for regulations

In the light of the information and data acquired pursuant to article 200, States shall cooperate, directly or through competent international organizations, in establishing appropriate scientific criteria for the formulation and elaboration of rules, standards and recommended practices and procedures for the prevention, reduction and control of pollution of the marine environment.

SECTION 3. TECHNICAL ASSISTANCE

ARTICLE 202

Scientific and technical assistance to developing States

States shall, directly or through competent international organizations:

(a) promote programmes of scientific, educational, technical and other assistance to developing States for the protection and preservation of the marine environment and the prevention, reduction and control of marine pollution. Such assistance shall include, *inter alia*:

(i) training of their scientific and technical personnel,

(ii) facilitating their participation in relevant international programmes,

(iii) supplying them with necessary equipment and facilities,

(iv) enhancing their capacity to manufacture such equipment,

(v) advice on and developing facilities for research, monitoring, educational and other programmes;

(b) provide appropriate assistance, especially to developing States, for the minimization of the effects of major incidents which may cause serious pollution of the marine environment;

(c) provide appropriate assistance, especially to developing States, concerning the preparation of environmental assessments.

ARTICLE 203

Preferential treatment for developing States

Developing States shall, for the purposes of prevention, reduction and control of pollution of the marine environment or minimization of its effects, be granted preference by international organizations in:

(a) the allocation of appropriate funds and technical assistance; and

(b) the utilization of their specialized services.

SECTION 4. MONITORING AND ENVIRONMENTAL ASSESSMENT

ARTICLE 204

Monitoring of the risks or effects of pollution

1. States shall, consistent with the rights of other States, endeavour, as far as practicable, directly or through the competent international organizations, to observe, measure, evaluate and analyse, by recognized scientific methods, the risks or effects of pollution of the marine environment.
2. In particular, States shall keep under surveillance the effects of any activities which they permit or in which they engage in order to determine whether these activities are likely to pollute the marine environment.

ARTICLE 205

Publication of reports

States shall publish reports of the results obtained pursuant to article 204 or provide such reports, at appropriate intervals, to the competent international organizations, which should make them available to all States.

ARTICLE 206

Assessment of potential effects of activities

When States have reasonable grounds for believing that planned activities under their jurisdiction or control may cause substantial pollution of or significant and harmful changes to the marine environment, they shall, as far as practicable, assess the potential effects of such activities on the marine environment and shall communicate reports of the results of such assessments in the manner provided in article 205.

SECTION 5. INTERNATIONAL RULES AND NATIONAL LEGISLATION TO PREVENT, REDUCE AND CONTROL POLLUTION OF THE MARINE ENVIRONMENT

ARTICLE 207

Pollution from land-based sources

1. States shall adopt laws and regulations to prevent, reduce and control pollution of the marine environment

from land-based sources, including rivers, estuaries, pipelines and outfall structures, taking into account internationally agreed rules, standards and recommended practices and procedures.

2. States shall take other measures as may be necessary to prevent, reduce and control such pollution.
3. States shall endeavour to harmonize their policies in this connection at the appropriate regional level.
4. States, acting especially through competent international organizations or diplomatic conference, shall endeavour to establish global and regional rules, standards and recommended practices and procedures to prevent, reduce and control pollution of the marine environment from land-based sources, taking into account characteristic regional features, the economic capacity of developing States and their need for economic development. Such rules, standards and recommended practices and procedures shall be re-examined from time to time as necessary.
5. Laws, regulations, measures, rules, standards and recommended practices and procedures referred to in paragraphs 1, 2 and 4 shall include those designed to minimize, to the fullest extent possible, the release of toxic, harmful or noxious substances, especially those which are persistent, into the marine environment.

ARTICLE 208

Pollution from seabed activities subject to national jurisdiction

1. Coastal States shall adopt laws and regulations to prevent, reduce and control pollution of the marine environment arising from or in connection with seabed activities subject to their jurisdiction and from artificial islands, installations and structures under their jurisdiction, pursuant to articles 60 and 80.
2. States shall take other measures as may be necessary to prevent, reduce and control such pollution.
3. Such laws, regulations and measures shall be no less effective than international rules, standards and recommended practices and procedures.

4. States shall endeavour to harmonize their policies in this connection at the appropriate regional level.
5. States, acting especially through competent international organizations or diplomatic conference, shall establish global and regional rules, standards and recommended practices and procedures to prevent, reduce and control pollution of the marine environment referred to in paragraph 1. Such rules, standards and recommended practices and procedures shall be re-examined from time to time as necessary.

ARTICLE 209

Pollution from activities in the Area

1. International rules, regulations and procedures shall be established in accordancc with Part XI to prevent, reduce and control pollution of the marine environment from activities in the Area. Such rules, regulations and procedures shall be re-examined from time to time as necessary.
2. Subject to the relevant provisions of this section, States shall adopt laws and regulations to prevent, reduce and control pollution of the marine environment from activities in the Area undertaken by vessels, installations, structures and other devices flying their flag or of their registry or operating under their authority, as the case may be. The requirements of such laws and regulations shall be no less effective than the international rules, regulations and procedures referred to in paragraph 1.

ARTICLE 210

Pollution by dumping

1. States shall adopt laws and regulations to prevent, reduce and control pollution of the marine environment by dumping.
2. States shall take other measures as may be necessary to prevent, reduce and control such pollution.
3. Such laws, regulations and measures shall ensure that dumping is not carried out without the permission of the competent authorities of States.

4. States, acting especially through competent international organizations or diplomatic conference, shall endeavour to establish global and regional rules, standards and recommended practices and procedures to prevent, reduce and control such pollution. Such rules, standards and recommended practices and procedures shall be re-examined from time to time as necessary.
5. Dumping within the territorial sea and the exclusive economic zone or onto the continental shelf shall not be carried out without the express prior approval of the coastal State, which has the right to permit, regulate and control such dumping after due consideration of the matter with other States which by reason of their geographical situation may be adversely affected thereby.
6. National laws, regulations and measures shall be no less effective in preventing, reducing and controlling such pollution than the global rules and standards.

ARTICLE 211

Pollution from vessels

1. States, acting through the competent international organization or general diplomatic conference, shall establish international rules and standards to prevent, reduce and control pollution of the marine environment from vessels and promote the adoption, in the same manner, wherever appropriate, of routing systems designed to minimize the threat of accidents which might cause pollution of the marine environment, including the coastline, and pollution damage to the related interests of coastal States. Such rules and standards shall, in the same manner, be re-examined from time to time as necessary.
2. States shall adopt laws and regulations for the prevention, reduction and control of pollution of the marine environment from vessels flying their flag or of their registry. Such laws and regulations shall at least have the same effect as that of generally accepted international rules and standards established through the competent international organization or general diplomatic conference.

3. States which establish particular requirements for the prevention, reduction and control of pollution of the marine environment as a condition for the entry of foreign vessels into their ports or internal waters or for a call at their off-shore terminals shall give due publicity to such requirements and shall communicate them to the competent international organization. Whenever such requirements are established in identical form by two or more coastal States in an endeavour to harmonize policy, the communication shall indicate which States are participating in such cooperative arrangements. Every State shall require the master of a vessel flying its flag or of its registry, when navigating within the territorial sea of a State participating in such cooperative arrangements, to furnish, upon the request of that State, information as to whether it is proceeding to a State of the same region participating in such cooperative arrangements and, if so, to indicate whether it complies with the port entry requirements of that State. This article is without prejudice to the continued exercise by a vessel of its right of innocent passage or to the application of article 25, paragraph 2.
4. Coastal States may, in the exercise of their sovereignty within their territorial sea, adopt laws and regulations for the prevention, reduction and control of marine pollution from foreign vessels, including vessels exercising the right of innocent passage. Such laws and regulations shall, in accordance with Part II, section 3, not hamper innocent passage of foreign vessels.
5. Coastal States, for the purpose of enforcement, as provided for in section 6, may in respect of their exclusive economic zones adopt laws and regulations for the prevention, reduction and control of pollution from vessels conforming to and giving effect to generally accepted international rules and standards established through the competent international organization or general diplomatic conference.
6. (a) Where the international rules and standards, referred to in paragraph 1, are inadequate to meet special circumstances and coastal States have reasonable

grounds for believing that a particular, clearly defined area of their respective exclusive economic zones is an area where the adoption of special mandatory measures for the prevention of pollution from vessels is required for recognized technical reasons in relation to its oceanographical and ecological conditions, as well as its utilization or the protection of its resources and the particular character of its traffic, the coastal States, after appropriate consultations through the competent international organization with any other States concerned, may, for that area, direct a communication to that organization, submitting scientific and technical evidence in support and information on necessary reception facilities. Within 12 months after receiving such a communication, the organization shall determine whether the conditions in that area correspond to the requirements set out above. If the organization so determines, the coastal States may, for that area, adopt laws and regulations for the prevention, reduction and control of pollution from vessels implementing such international rules and standards or navigational practices as are made applicable, through the organization, for special areas. These laws and regulations shall not become applicable to foreign vessels until 15 months after the submission of the communication to the organization.

(b) The coastal States shall publish the limits of any such particular, clearly defined area.

(c) If the coastal States intend to adopt additional laws and regulations for the same area for the prevention, reduction and control of pollution from vessels, they shall, when submitting the aforesaid communication, at the same time notify the organization thereof. Such additional laws and regulations may relate to discharges or navigational practices but shall not require foreign vessels to observe design, construction, manning or equipment standards other than generally accepted international rules and standards; they shall become applicable to foreign vessels 15 months after the submission of the communication to the organization, provided that the organization agrees within 12 months after the submission of the communication.

7. The international rules and standards referred to in this article should include, *inter alia,* those relating to prompt notification to coastal States, whose coastline or related interests may be affected by incidents, including maritime casualties, which involve discharges or probability of discharges.

ARTICLE 212

Pollution from or through the atmosphere

1. States shall adopt laws and regulations to prevent, reduce and control pollution of the marine environment from or through the atmosphere, applicable to the air space under their sovereignty and to vessels flying their flag or vessels or aircraft of their registry, taking into account internationally agreed rules, standards and recommended practices and procedures and the safety of air navigation.
2. States shall take other measures as may be necessary to prevent, reduce and control such pollution.
3. States, acting especially through competent international organizations or diplomatic conference, shall endeavour to establish global and regional rules, standards and recommended practices and procedures to prevent, reduce and control such pollution.

SECTION 6. ENFORCEMENT

ARTICLE 213

Enforcement with respect to pollution from land-based sources

States shall enforce their laws and regulations adopted in accordance with article 207 and shall adopt laws and regulations and take other measures necessary to implement applicable international rules and standards established through competent international organizations or diplomatic conference to prevent, reduce and control pollution of the marine environment from land-based sources.

ARTICLE 214

Enforcement with respect to pollution from seabed activities

States shall enforce their laws and regulations adopted in accordance with article 208 and shall adopt laws and regulations and take other measures necessary to implement applicable international rules and standards established through competent international organizations or diplomatic conference to prevent, reduce and control pollution of the marine environment arising from or in connection with seabed activities subject to their jurisdiction and from artificial islands, installations and structures under their jurisdiction, pursuant to articles 60 and 80.

ARTICLE 215

Enforcement with respect to pollution from activities in the Area

Enforcement of international rules, regulations and procedures established in accordance with Part XI to prevent, reduce and control pollution of the marine environment from activities in the Area shall be governed by that Part.

ARTICLE 216

Enforcement with respect to pollution by dumping

1. Laws and regulations adopted in accordance with this Convention and applicable international rules and standards established through competent international organizations or diplomatic conference for the prevention, reduction and control of pollution of the marine environment by dumping shall be enforced:
   (a) by the coastal State with regard to dumping within its territorial sea or its exclusive economic zone or onto its continental shelf;
   (b) by the flag State with regard to vessels flying its flag or vessels or aircraft of its registry; and
   (c) by any State with regard to acts of loading of wastes or other matter occurring within its territory or at its off-shore terminals.

2. No State shall be obliged by virtue of this article to institute proceedings when another State has already instituted proceedings in accordance with this article.

ARTICLE 217

Enforcement by flag States

1. States shall ensure compliance by vessels flying their flag or of their registry with applicable international rules and standards, established through the competent international organization or general diplomatic conference, and with their laws and regulations adopted in accordance with this Convention for the prevention, reduction and control of pollution of the marine environment from vessels and shall accordingly adopt laws and regulations and take other measures necessary for their implementation. Flag States shall provide for the effective enforcement of such rules, standards, laws and regulations, irrespective of where a violation occurs.
2. States shall, in particular, take appropriate measures in order to ensure that vessels flying their flag or of their registry are prohibited from sailing, until they can proceed to sea in compliance with the requirements of the international rules and standards referred to in paragraph 1, including requirements in respect of design, construction, equipment and manning of vessels.
3. States shall ensure that vessels flying their flag or of their registry carry on board certificates required by and issued pursuant to international rules and standards referred to in paragraph 1. States shall ensure that vessels flying their flag are periodically inspected in order to verify that such certificates are in conformity with the actual condition of the vessels. These certificates shall be accepted by other States as evidence of the condition of the vessels and shall be regarded as having the same force as certificates issued by them, unless there are clear grounds for believing that the condition of the vessel does not correspond substantially with the particulars of the certificates.
4. If a vessel commits a violation of rules and standards established through the competent international

organization or general diplomatic conference, the flag State, without prejudice to articles 218, 220 and 228, shall provide for immediate investigation and, where appropriate, institute proceedings in respect of the alleged violation irrespective of where the violation occurred or where the pollution caused by such violation has occurred or has been spotted.

5. Flag States conducting an investigation of the violation may request the assistance of any other State whose cooperation could be useful in clarifying the circumstances of the case. States shall endeavour to meet appropriate requests of flag States.
6. States shall, at the written request of any State, investigate any violation alleged to have been committed by vessels flying their flag. If satisfied that sufficient evidence is available to enable proceedings to be brought in respect of the alleged violation, flag States shall without delay institute such proceedings in accordance with their laws.
7. Flag States shall promptly inform the requesting State and the competent international organization of the action taken and its outcome. Such information shall be available to all States.
8. Penalties provided for by the laws and regulations of States for vessels flying their flag shall be adequate in severity to discourage violations wherever they occur.

ARTICLE 218

Enforcement by port States

1. When a vessel is voluntarily within a port or at an off-shore terminal of a State, that State may undertake investigations and, where the evidence so warrants, institute proceedings in respect of any discharge from that vessel outside the internal waters, territorial sea or exclusive economic zone of that State in violation of applicable international rules and standards established through the competent international organization or general diplomatic conference.
2. No proceedings, pursuant to paragraph 1, shall be

instituted in respect of a discharge violation in the internal waters, territorial sea or exclusive economic zone of another State unless requested by that State, the flag State, or a State damaged or threatened by the discharge violation, or unless the violation has caused or is likely to cause pollution in the internal waters, territorial sea or exclusive economic zone of the State instituting the proceedings.

3. When a vessel is voluntarily within a port or at an off-shore terminal of a State, that State shall, as far as practicable, comply with requests from any State for investigation of a discharge violation referred to in paragraph 1, believed to have occurred in, caused, or threatened damage to the internal waters, territorial sea or exclusive economic zone of the requesting State. It shall likewise, as far as practicable, comply with requests from the flag State for investigation of such a violation, irrespective of where the violation occurred.

4. The records of the investigation carried out by a port State, pursuant to this article, shall be transmitted upon request to the flag State or to the coastal State. Any proceedings instituted by the port State on the basis of such an investigation may, subject to section 7, be suspended at the request of the coastal State when the violation has occurred within its internal waters, territorial sea or exclusive economic zone. The evidence and records of the case, together with any bond or other financial security posted with the authorities of the port State, shall in that event be transmitted to the coastal State. Such transmittal shall preclude the continuation of proceedings in the port State.

ARTICLE 219

Measures relating to seaworthiness of vessels to avoid pollution

Subject to section 7, States which, upon request or on their own initiative, have ascertained that a vessel within one of their ports or at one of their off-shore terminals is in violation of applicable international rules and standards relating to seaworthiness of vessels, and thereby threatens damage to the marine environment shall, as far as practicable, take administrative measures to prevent the vessel from sailing. Such States may permit the vessel to proceed only to the nearest appropriate repair yard and, upon removal of the causes of the violation, shall permit the vessel to continue immediately.

ARTICLE 220

Enforcement by coastal States

1. When a vessel is voluntarily within a port or at an off-shore terminal of a State, that State may, subject to section 7, institute proceedings in respect of any violation of its laws and regulations adopted in accordance with this Convention or applicable international rules and standards for the prevention, reduction and control of pollution from vessels when the violation has occurred within the territorial sea or the exclusive economic zone of that State.
2. Where there are clear grounds for believing that a vessel navigating in the territorial sea of a State has, during its passage therein, violated laws and regulations of that State adopted in accordance with this Convention or applicable international rules and standards for the prevention, reduction and control of pollution from vessels, that State, without prejudice to the application of the relevant provisions of Part II, section 3, may undertake physical inspection of the vessel relating to the violation and may, where the evidence so warrants, institute proceedings, including detention of the vessel, in accordance with its laws, subject to the provisions of section 7.
3. Where there are clear grounds for believing that a vessel navigating in the exclusive economic zone or the territorial sea of a State has, in the exclusive economic zone, committed a violation of applicable international rules and standards for the prevention, reduction and control of pollution from vessels or laws and regulations of that State, conforming and giving effect to such rules and standards, that State may require the vessel to give information regarding its identity and port of registry, its last and its next port of call and other relevant

information required to establish whether a violation has occurred.

4. States shall adopt laws and regulations and take other measures so that vessels flying their flag comply with requests for information pursuant to paragraph 3.

5. Where there are clear grounds for believing that a vessel navigating in the exclusive economic zone or the territorial sea of a State has, in the exclusive economic zone, committed a violation referred to in paragraph 3 resulting in a substantial discharge causing or threatening significant pollution of the marine environment, that State may undertake physical inspection of the vessel for matters relating to the violation if the vessel has refused to give information or if the information supplied by the vessel is manifestly at variance with the evident factual situation and if the circumstances of the case justify such inspection.

6. Where there is clear objective evidence that a vessel navigating in the exclusive economic zone or the territorial sea of a State has, in the exclusive economic zone, committed a violation referred to in paragraph 3 resulting in a discharge causing major damage or threat of major damage to the coastline or related interests of the coastal State, or to any resources of its territorial sea or exclusive economic zone, that State may, subject to section 7, provided that the evidence so warrants, institute proceedings, including detention of the vessel, in accordance with its laws.

7. Notwithstanding the provisions of paragraph 6, whenever appropriate procedures have been established, either through the competent international organization or as otherwise agreed, whereby compliance with requirements for bonding or other appropriate financial security has been assured, the coastal State if bound by such procedures shall allow the vessel to proceed.

8. The provisions of paragraphs 3, 4, 5, 6 and 7 also apply in respect of national laws and regulations adopted pursuant to article 211, paragraph 6.

ARTICLE 221

Measures to avoid pollution arising from maritime casualties

1. Nothing in this Part shall prejudice the right of States, pursuant to international law, both customary and conventional, to take and enforce measures beyond the territorial sea proportionate to the actual or threatened damage to protect their coastline or related interests, including fishing, from pollution or threat of pollution following upon a maritime casualty or acts relating to such a casualty, which may reasonably be expected to result in major harmful consequences.
2. For the purposes of this article, "maritime casualty" means a collision of vessels, stranding or other incident of navigation, or other occurrence on board a vessel or external to it resulting in material damage or imminent threat of material damage to a vessel or cargo.

ARTICLE 222

Enforcement with respect to pollution from or through the atmosphere

States shall enforce, within the air space under their sovereignty or with regard to vessels flying their flag, or vessels or aircraft of their registry, their laws and regulations adopted in accordance with article 212, paragraph 1, and with other provisions of this Convention and shall adopt laws and regulations and take other measures necessary to implement applicable international rules and standards established through competent international organizations or diplomatic conference to prevent, reduce and control pollution of the marine environment from or through the atmosphere, in conformity with all relevant international rules and standards concerning the safety of air navigation.

SECTION 7. SAFEGUARDS

ARTICLE 223

Measures to facilitate proceedings

In proceedings instituted pursuant to this Part, States shall take measures to facilitate the hearing of witnesses and the admission of evidence submitted by authorities of another

State, or by the competent international organization, and shall facilitate the attendance, at such proceedings, of official representatives of the competent international organization, the flag State and any State affected by pollution arising out of any violation. The official representatives attending such proceedings shall have such rights and duties as may be provided under national laws and regulations or international law.

ARTICLE 224

Exercise of the powers of enforcement

The powers of enforcement against foreign vessels, under this Part may only be exercised by officials or by warships, military aircraft, or other ships or aircraft clearly marked and identifiable as being on government service and authorized to that effect.

ARTICLE 225

Duty to avoid adverse consequences in the exercise of the powers of enforcement

In the exercise under this Convention of their powers of enforcement against foreign vessels, States shall not endanger the safety of navigation or otherwise create any hazard to a vessel, or bring it to an unsafe port or anchorage, or expose the marine environment to an unreasonable risk.

ARTICLE 226

Investigation of foreign vessels

1. (a) States shall not delay a foreign vessel longer than is essential for purposes of the investigations provided for in articles 216, 218 and 220. Any physical inspection of a foreign vessel shall be limited to an examination of such certificates, records or other documents as the vessel is required to carry by generally accepted international rules and standards or of any similar documents which it is carrying; further physical inspection of the vessel may be undertaken only after such an examination and only when:

    (i) there are clear grounds for believing that the condition of the vessel, or its equipment does not correspond substantially with the particulars of those documents,

(ii) the contents of such documents are not sufficient to confirm or verify a suspected violation, or

(iii) the vessel is not carrying valid certificates and records.

(b) If the investigation indicates a violation of applicable laws and regulations or international rules and standards for the protection and preservation of the marine environment, release shall be made promptly subject to reasonable procedures such as bonding or other appropriate financial security.

(c) Without prejudice to applicable international rules and standards relating to the seaworthiness of vessels, the release of a vessel may, whenever it would present an unreasonable threat of damage to the marine environment, be refused or made conditional upon proceeding to the nearest appropriate repair yard. Where release has been refused or made conditional, the flag State of the vessel must be promptly notified, and may seek release of the vessel in accordance with Part XV.

2. States shall cooperate to develop procedures for the avoidance of unnecessary physical inspection of vessels at sea.

ARTICLE 227

Non-discrimination with respect to foreign vessels

In exercising their rights and performing their duties under this Part, States shall not discriminate in form or in fact against vessels of any other State.

ARTICLE 228

Suspension and restrictions on institution of proceedings

1. Proceedings to impose penalties in respect of any violation of applicable laws and regulations or international rules and standards relating to the prevention, reduction and control of pollution from

vessels committed by a foreign vessel beyond the territorial sea of the State instituting proceedings shall be suspended upon the taking of proceedings to impose penalties in respect of corresponding charges by the flag State within six months of the date on which proceedings were first instituted, unless those proceedings relate to a case of major damage to the coastal State or the flag State in question has repeatedly disregarded its obligation to enforce effectively the applicable international rules and standards in respect of violations committed by its vessels. The flag State shall, in due course, make available to the State previously instituting proceedings a full dossier of the case and the records of the proceedings, whenever the flag State has requested the suspension of proceedings in accordance with this article. When proceedings instituted by the flag State have been brought to a conclusion, the suspended proceedings shall be terminated. Upon payment of costs incurred in respect of such proceedings, any bond posted or other financial security provided in connection with the suspended proceedings shall be released by the coastal State.

2. Proceedings to impose penalties on foreign vessels shall not be instituted after the expiry of three years from the date on which the violation was committed, and shall not be taken by any State in the event of proceedings having been instituted by another State subject to the provisions set out in paragraph 1.
3. The provisions of this article are without prejudice to the right of the flag State to take any measures, including proceedings to impose penalties, according to its laws irrespective of prior proceedings by another State.

ARTICLE 229

Institution of civil proceedings

Nothing in this Convention affects the institution of civil proceedings in respect of any claim for loss or damage resulting from pollution of the marine environment.

ARTICLE 230

Monetary penalties and the observance of recognized rights of the accused

1. Monetary penalties only may be imposed with respect to violations of national laws and regulations or applicable international rules and standards for the prevention, reduction and control of pollution of the marine environment, committed by foreign vessels beyond the territorial sea.
2. Monetary penalties only may be imposed with respect to violations of national laws and regulations or applicable international rules and standards for the prevention, reduction and control of pollution of the marine environment, committed by foreign vessels in the territorial sea, except in the case of a wilful and serious act of pollution in the territorial sea.
3. In the conduct of proceedings in respect of such violations committed by a foreign vessel which may result in the imposition of penalties, recognized rights of the accused shall be observed.

ARTICLE 231

Notification to the flag State and other States concerned

States shall promptly notify the flag State and any other State concerned of any measures taken, pursuant to section 6, against foreign vessels, and shall submit to the flag State all official reports concerning such measures. However, with respect to violations committed in the territorial sea, the foregoing obligations of the coastal State apply only to such measures as are taken in proceedings. The diplomatic agents or consular officers and where possible the maritime authority of the flag State, shall be immediately informed of any such measures taken pursuant to section 6 against foreign vessels.

ARTICLE 232

Liability of States arising from enforcement measures

States shall be liable for damage or loss attributable to them arising from measures taken, pursuant to section 6, when such measures are unlawful or exceed those reasonably required in the light of available information. States shall provide for recourse in their courts for actions in respect of such damage or loss.

ARTICLE 233

Safeguards with respect to straits used for international navigation

Nothing in sections 5, 6 and 7 affects the legal regime of straits used for international navigation. However, if a foreign ship, other than those referred to in section 10, has committed a violation of the laws and regulations referred to in article 42, paragraph 1(a) and (b), causing or threatening major damage to the marine environment of the straits, the States bordering the straits may take appropriate enforcement measures and if so shall respect *mutatis mutandis* the provisions of this section.

SECTION 8. ICE-COVERED AREAS

ARTICLE 234

Ice-covered areas

Coastal States have the right to adopt and enforce non-discriminatory laws and regulations for the prevention, reduction and control of marine pollution from vessels in ice-covered areas within the limits of the exclusive economic zone, where particularly severe climatic conditions and the presence of ice covering such areas for most of the year create obstructions or exceptional hazards to navigation, and pollution of the marine environment could cause major harm to or irreversible disturbance of the ecological balance. Such laws and regulations shall have due regard to navigation and the protection and preservation of the marine environment based on the best available scientific evidence.

SECTION 9. RESPONSIBILITY AND LIABILITY

ARTICLE 235

Responsibility and liability

1. States are responsible for the fulfilment of their international obligations concerning the protection and preservation of the marine environment. They shall be liable in accordance with international law.

2. States shall ensure that recourse is available in accordance with their legal systems for prompt and adequate compensation or other relief in respect of damage caused by pollution of the marine environment by natural or juridical persons under their jurisdiction.
3. With the objective of assuring prompt and adequate compensation in respect of all damage caused by pollution of the marine environment, States shall cooperate in the implementation of existing international law and the further development of international law relating to responsibility and liability for the assessment of and compensation for damage and the settlement of related disputes, as well as, where appropriate, development of criteria and procedures for payment of adequate compensation, such as compulsory insurance or compensation funds.

SECTION 10. SOVEREIGN IMMUNITY

ARTICLE 236

Sovereign immunity

The provisions of this Convention regarding the protection and preservation of the marine environment do not apply to any warship, naval auxiliary, other vessels or aircraft owned or operated by a State and used, for the time being, only on government non-commercial service. However, each State shall ensure, by the adoption of appropriate measures not impairing operations or operational capabilities of such vessels or aircraft owned or operated by it, that such vessels or aircraft act in a manner consistent, so far as is reasonable and practicable, with this Convention.

SECTION 11. OBLIGATIONS UNDER OTHER CONVENTIONS ON THE PROTECTION AND PRESERVATION OF THE MARINE ENVIRONMENT

ARTICLE 237

Obligations under other conventions on the protection and preservation of the marine environment

1. The provisions of this Part are without prejudice to the specific obligations assumed by States under special

conventions and agreements concluded previously which relate to the protection and preservation of the marine environment and to agreements which may be concluded in furtherance of the general principles set forth in this Convention.

2. Specific obligations assumed by States under special conventions, with respect to the protection and preservation of the marine environment, should be carried out in a manner consistent with the general principles and objectives of this Convention.

LAW OF SEA CONVENTION, 1982

PART-XIII

Marine Scientific Research

SECTION 1. GENERAL PROVISIONS

ARTICLE 238

Right to conduct marine scientific research

All States, irrespective of their geographical location, and competent international organizations have the right to conduct marine scientific research subject to the rights and duties of other States as provided for in this Convention.

ARTICLE 239

Promotion of marine scientific research

States and competent international organizations shall promote and facilitate the development and conduct of marine scientific research in accordance with this Convention.

ARTICLE 240

General principles for the conduct of marine scientific research

In the conduct of marine scientific research the following principles shall apply:

(a) marine scientific research shall be conducted exclusively for peaceful purposes;

(b) marine scientific research shall be conducted with appropriate scientific methods and means compatible with this Convention;

(c) marine scientific research shall not unjustifiably interfere with other legitimate uses of the sea compatible with this Convention and shall be duly respected in the course of such uses;

(d) marine scientific research shall be conducted in compliance with all relevant regulations adopted in conformity with this Convention including those for the protection and preservation of the marine environment.

ARTICLE 241

Non-recognition of marine scientific research activities as the legal basis for claims

Marine scientific research activities shall not constitute the legal basis for any claim to any part of the marine environment or its resources.

SECTION 2. INTERNATIONAL COOPERATION

ARTICLE 242

Promotion of international cooperation

1. States and competent international organizations shall, in accordance with the principle of respect for sovereignty and jurisdiction and on the basis of mutual benefit, promote international cooperation in marine scientific research for peaceful purposes.
2. In this context, without prejudice to the rights and duties of States under this Convention, a State, in the application of this Part, shall provide, as appropriate, other States with a reasonable opportunity to obtain from it, or with its cooperation, information necessary to prevent and control damage to the health and safety of persons and to the marine environment.

ARTICLE 243

Creation of favourable conditions

States and competent international organizations shall cooperate, through the conclusion of bilateral and multilateral agreements, to create favourable conditions for the conduct of marine scientific research in the marine environment and to integrate the efforts of scientists in studying the essence of phenomena and processes occurring in the marine environment and the interrelations between them.

ARTICLE 244

Publication and dissemination of information and knowledge

1. States and competent international organizations shall, in accordance with this Convention, make available by publication and dissemination through appropriate channels information on proposed major programmes

and their objectives as well as knowledge resulting from marine scientific research.

2. For this purpose, States, both individually and in cooperation with other States and with competent international organizations, shall actively promote the flow of scientific data and information and the transfer of knowledge resulting from marine scientific research, especially to developing States, as well as the strengthening of the autonomous marine scientific research capabilities of developing States through, *inter alia,* programmes to provide adequate education and training of their technical and scientific personnel.

SECTION 3. CONDUCT AND PROMOTION OF MARINE SCIENTIFIC RESEARCH

ARTICLE 245

Marine scientific research in the territorial sea

Coastal States, in the exercise of their sovereignty, have the exclusive right to regulate, authorize and conduct marine scientific research in their territorial sea. Marine scientific research therein shall be conducted only with the express consent of and under the conditions set forth by the coastal State.

ARTICLE 246

Marine scientific research in the exclusive economic zone and on the continental shelf

1. Coastal States, in the exercise of their jurisdiction, have the right to regulate, authorize and conduct marine scientific research in their exclusive economic zone and on their continental shelf in accordance with the relevant provisions of this Convention.
2. Marine scientific research in the exclusive economic zone and on the continental shelf shall be conducted with the consent of the coastal State.
3. Coastal States shall, in normal circumstances, grant their consent for marine scientific research projects by other States or competent international organizations in their exclusive economic zone or on their continental shelf to be carried out, in accordance with this

Convention, exclusively for peaceful purposes and in order to increase scientific knowledge of the marine environment for the benefit of all mankind. To this end, coastal States shall establish rules and procedures ensuring that such consent will not be delayed or denied unreasonably.

4. For the purposes of applying paragraph 3, normal circumstances may exist in spite of the absence of diplomatic relations between the coastal State and the researching State.

5. Coastal States may, however, in their discretion withhold their consent to the conduct of a marine scientific research project of another State or competent international organization in the exclusive economic zone or on the continental shelf of the coastal State if that project:

   (a) is of direct significance for the exploration and exploitation of natural resources, whether living or non-living;

   (b) involves drilling into the continental shelf, the use of explosives or the introduction of harmful substances into the marine environment;

   (c) involves the construction, operation or use of artificial islands, installations and structures referred to in articles 60 and 80;

   (d) contains information communicated pursuant to article 248 regarding the nature and objectives of the project which is inaccurate or if the researching State or competent international organization has outstanding obligations to the coastal State from a prior research project.

6. Notwithstanding the provisions of paragraph 5, coastal States may not exercise their discretion to withhold consent under subparagraph (a) of that paragraph in respect of marine scientific research projects to be undertaken in accordance with the provisions of this Part on the continental shelf, beyond 200 nautical miles from the baselines from which the breadth of the territorial sea is measured, outside those specific areas

which coastal States may, at any time, publicly designate as areas in which exploitation or detailed exploratory operations focused on those areas are occurring or will occur within a reasonable period of time. Coastal States shall give reasonable notice of the designation of such areas, as well as any modifications thereto, but shall not be obliged to give details of the operations therein.

7. The provisions of paragraph 6 are without prejudice to the rights of coastal States over the continental shelf as established in article 77.

8. Marine scientific research activities referred to in this article shall not unjustifiably interfere with activities undertaken by coastal States in the exercise of their sovereign rights and jurisdiction provided for in this Convention.

ARTICLE 247

Marine scientific research projects undertaken by or under the auspices of international organizations

A coastal State which is a member of or has a bilateral agreement with an international organization, and in whose exclusive economic zone or on whose continental shelf that organization wants to carry out a marine scientific research project, directly or under its auspices, shall be deemed to have authorized the project to be carried out in conformity with the agreed specifications if that State approved the detailed project when the decision was made by the organization for the undertaking of the project, or is willing to participate in it, and has not expressed any objection within four months of notification of the project by the organization to the coastal State.

ARTICLE 248

Duty to provide information to the coastal State

States and competent international organizations which intend to undertake marine scientific research in the exclusive economic zone or on the continental shelf of a coastal State shall, not less than six months in advance of the expected starting date of the marine scientific research project, provide that State with a full description of —

(a) the nature and objectives of the project;

(b) the method and means to be used, including name, tonnage, type and class of vessels, and a description of scientific equipment;

(c) the precise geographical areas in which the project is to be conducted;

(d) the expected date of first appearance and final departure of the research vessels, or deployment of the equipment and its removal, as appropriate;

(e) the name of the sponsoring institution, its director, and the person in charge of the project; and

(f) the extent to which it is considered that the coastal State should be able to participate or to be represented in the project.

ARTICLE 249

Duty to comply with certain conditions

1. States and competent international organizations when undertaking marine scientific research in the exclusive economic zone or on the continental shelf of a coastal State shall comply with the following conditions:

   (a) ensure the right of the coastal State, if it so desires, to participate or be represented in the marine scientific research project, especially on board research vessels and other craft or scientific research installations, when practicable, without payment of any remuneration to the scientists of the coastal State and without obligation to contribute towards the costs of the project;

   (b) provide the coastal State, at its request, with preliminary reports, as soon as practicable, and with the final results and conclusions after the completion of the research;

   (c) undertake to provide access for the coastal State, at its request, to all data and samples derived from the marine scientific research project and likewise, to furnish it with data which may be copied and samples which may be divided without detriment to their scientific value;

(d) if requested, provide the coastal State with an assessment of such data, samples and research results or provide assistance in their assessment or interpretation;

(e) ensure, subject to paragraph 2, that the research results are made internationally available through appropriate national or international channels, as soon as practicable;

(f) inform the coastal State immediately of any major change in the research programme;

(g) unless otherwise agreed, remove the scientific research installations or equipment once the research is completed.

2. This article is without prejudice to the conditions established by the laws and regulations of the coastal State for the exercise of its discretion to grant or withhold consent pursuant to article 246, paragraph 5, including requiring prior agreement for making internationally available the research results of a project of direct significance for the exploration and exploitation of natural resources.

ARTICLE 250

Communications concerning marine scientific research projects

Communications concerning the marine scientific research projects shall be made through appropriate official channels, unless otherwise agreed.

ARTICLE 251

General criteria and guidelines

States shall seek to promote through competent international organizations, the establishment of general criteria and guidelines to assist States in ascertaining the nature and implications of marine scientific research.

ARTICLE 252

Implied consent

States or competent international organizations may proceed with a marine scientific research project six months after the date upon which the information required pursuant to article 248 was provided to the coastal State, unless within four months of the receipt of the communication containing such information the coastal State has informed the State or organization conducting the research that:

(a) it has withheld its consent under the provisions of article 246; or

(b) the information given by that State or competent international organization regarding the nature or objectives of the project does not conform to the manifestly evident facts; or

(c) it requires supplementary information relevant to conditions and the information provided for under articles 248 and 249; or

(d) outstanding obligations exist with respect to a previous marine scientific research project carried out by that State or organization, with regard to conditions established in article 249.

ARTICLE 253

Suspension or cessation of marine scientific research activities

1. A coastal State shall have the right to require the suspension of any marine scientific research activities in progress within its exclusive economic zone or on its continental shelf if:

   (a) the research activities are not being conducted in accordance with the information communicated as provided under article 248 upon which the consent of the coastal State was based; or

   (b) the State or competent international organization conducting the research activities fails to comply with the provisions of article 249 concerning the rights of the coastal State with respect to the marine scientific research project.

2. A coastal State shall have the right to require the cessation of any marine scientific research activities in case of any non-compliance with the provisions of article 248 which amounts to a major change in the research project or the research activities.
3. A coastal State may also require cessation of marine scientific research activities if any of the situations contemplated in paragraph 1 are not rectified within a reasonable period of time.
4. Following notification by the coastal State of its decision to order suspension or cessation, States or competent international organizations authorized to conduct marine scientific research activities shall terminate the research activities that are the subject of such a notification.
5. An order of suspension under paragraph 1 shall be lifted by the coastal State and the marine scientific research activities allowed to continue once the researching State or competent international organization has complied with the conditions required under articles 248 and 249.

ARTICLE 254

Rights of neighbouring landlocked and geographically disadvantaged States

1. States and competent international organizations which have submitted to a coastal State a project to undertake marine scientific research referred to in article 246, paragraph 3, shall give notice to the neighbouring landlocked and geographically disadvantaged States of the proposed research project, and shall notify the coastal State thereof.
2. After the consent has been given for the proposed marine scientific research project by the coastal State concerned, in accordance with article 246 and other relevant provisions of this Convention, States and competent international organizations undertaking such a project shall provide to the neighbouring landlocked and geographically disadvantaged States, at their request and when appropriate, relevant information as specified in article 248 and article 249, paragraph 1.

3. The neighbouring landlocked and geographically disadvantaged States referred to above shall, at their request, be given the opportunity to participate, whenever feasible, in the proposed marine scientific research project through qualified experts appointed by them and not objected to by the coastal State, in accordance with the conditions agreed for the project, in conformity with the provisions of this Convention, between the coastal State concerned and the State or competent international organizations conducting the marine scientific research.
4. States and competent international organizations referred to in paragraph 1 shall provide to the above-mentioned landlocked and geographically disadvantaged States, at their request, the information and assistance specified in article 249, paragraph 1(d), subject to the provisions of article 249, paragraph 2.

ARTICLE 255

Measures to facilitate marine scientific research and assist research vessels

States shall endeavour to adopt reasonable rules, regulations and procedures to promote and facilitate marine scientific research conducted in accordance with this Convention beyond their territorial sea and, as appropriate, to facilitate, subject to the provisions of their laws and regulations, access to their harbours and promote assistance for marine scientific research vessels which comply with the relevant provisions of this Part.

ARTICLE 256

Marine scientific research in the Area

All States, irrespective of their geographical location, and competent international organizations have the right, in conformity with the provisions of Part XI, to conduct marine scientific research in the Area.

ARTICLE 257

Marine scientific research in the water column beyond the exclusive economic zone

All States, irrespective of their geographical location, and competent international organizations have the right, in conformity with this Convention, to conduct marine scientific research in the water column beyond the limits of the exclusive economic zone.

SECTION 4. SCIENTIFIC RESEARCH INSTALLATIONS OR EQUIPMENT IN THE MARINE ENVIRONMENT

ARTICLE 258

Deployment and use

The deployment and use of any type of scientific research installations or equipment in any area of the marine environment shall be subject to the same conditions as are prescribed in this Convention for the conduct of marine scientific research in any such area.

ARTICLE 259

Legal status

The installations or equipment referred to in this section do not possess the status of islands. They have no territorial sea of their own, and their presence does not affect the delimitation of the territorial sea, the exclusive economic zone or the continental shelf.

ARTICLE 260

Safety zones

Safety zones of a reasonable breadth not exceeding a distance of 500 metres may be created around scientific research installations, in accordance with the relevant provisions of this Convention. All States shall ensure that such safety zones are respected by their vessels.

ARTICLE 261

Non-interference with shipping routes

The deployment and use of any type of scientific research installations or equipment shall not constitute an obstacle to established international shipping routes.

ARTICLE 262

Identification markings and warning signals

Installations or equipment referred to in this section shall bear identification markings indicating the State of registry or the international organization to which they belong and shall have adequate internationally agreed warning signals to ensure safety at sea and the safety of air navigation, taking into account rules and standards established by competent international organizations.

SECTION 5. RESPONSIBILITY AND LIABILITY

ARTICLE 263

Responsibility and liability

1. States and competent international organizations shall be responsible for ensuring that marine scientific research, whether undertaken by them or on their behalf, is conducted in accordance with this Convention.
2. States and competent international organizations shall be responsible and liable for the measures they take in contravention of this Convention in respect of marine scientific research conducted by other States, their natural or juridical persons or by competent international organizations, and shall provide compensation for damage resulting from such measures.
3. States and competent international organizations shall be responsible and liable pursuant to article 235 for damage caused by pollution of the marine environment arising out of marine scientific research undertaken by them or on their behalf.

SECTION 6. SETTLEMENT OF DISPUTES AND INTERIM MEASURES

ARTICLE 264

Settlement of disputes

Disputes concerning the interpretation or application of the provisions of this Convention with regard to marine scientific research shall be settled in accordance with Part XV, sections 2 and 3.

ARTICLE 265

Interim measures

Pending settlement of a dispute in accordance with Part XV, sections 2 and 3, the State or the competent international organization authorized to conduct a marine scientific research project shall not allow research activities to commence or continue without the express consent of the coastal State concerned.

LAW OF SEA CONVENTION, 1982

PART-XIV

Development and Transfer of Marine Technology

SECTION 1. GENERAL PROVISIONS

ARTICLE 266

Promotion of the development and transfer of marine technology

1. States, directly or through competent international organizations, shall cooperate, in accordance with their capabilities, to promote actively the development and transfer of marine science and marine technology on fair and reasonable terms and conditions.
2. States shall promote the development of the marine scientific and technological capacity of States which may need and request technical assistance in this field, particularly developing States, including landlocked and geographically disadvantaged States, with regard to the exploration, exploitation, conservation and management of marine resources, the protection and preservation of the marine environment, marine scientific research and other activities in the marine environment compatible with this Convention, with a view to accelerating the social and economic development of the developing States.
3. States shall endeavour to foster favourable economic and legal conditions for the transfer of marine technology for the benefit of all parties concerned on an equitable basis.

ARTICLE 267

Protection of legitimate interests

States, in promoting cooperation pursuant to article 266, shall have due regard for all legitimate interests including, *inter alia*, the rights and duties of holders, suppliers and recipients of marine technology.

ARTICLE 268

Basic objectives

States, directly or through competent international organizations, shall promote:

(a) the acquisition, evaluation and dissemination of marine technological knowledge, and facilitate access to such information and data;

(b) the development of appropriate marine technology;

(c) the development of the necessary technological infrastructure to facilitate the transfer of marine technology;

(d) the development of human resources through training and education of nationals of developing States and countries and especially the nationals of the least developed among them; and

(e) international cooperation at all levels, particularly at the regional, subregional and bilateral levels.

ARTICLE 269

Measures to achieve the basic objectives

In order to achieve the objectives referred to in article 268, States, directly or through competent international organizations, shall endeavour, *inter alia*, to —

(a) establish programmes of technical cooperation for the effective transfer of all kinds of marine technology to States which may need and request technical assistance in this field, particularly the developing landlocked and geographically disadvantaged States, as well as other developing States which have not been able either to establish or develop their own technological capacity in marine science and in the exploration and exploitation of marine resources or to develop the infrastructure of such technology;

(b) promote favourable conditions for the conclusion of agreements, contracts and other similar arrangements, under equitable and reasonable conditions;

(c) hold conferences, seminars and symposia on scientific and technological subjects, in particular on policies and methods for the transfer of marine technology;

(d) promote the exchange of scientists and of technological and other experts; and

(e) undertake projects and promote joint ventures and other forms of bilateral and multilateral cooperation.

SECTION 2. INTERNATIONAL COOPERATION

ARTICLE 270

Ways and means of international cooperation

International cooperation for the development and transfer of marine technology shall be carried out, where feasible and appropriate, through existing bilateral, regional or multilateral programmes, and also through expanded and new programmes in order to facilitate marine scientific research, the transfer of marine technology, particularly in new fields, and appropriate international funding for ocean research and development.

ARTICLE 271

Guidelines, criteria and standards

States, directly or through competent international organizations, shall promote the establishment of generally accepted guidelines, criteria and standards for the transfer of marine technology on a bilateral basis or within the framework of international organizations and other fora, taking into account, in particular, the interests and needs of developing States.

ARTICLE 272

Coordination of international programmes

In the field of transfer of marine technology, States shall endeavour to ensure that competent international organizations coordinate their activities, including any regional or global programmes, taking into account the interests and needs of developing States, particularly landlocked and geographically disadvantaged States.

ARTICLE 273

Cooperation with international organizations and the Authority

States shall cooperate actively with competent international organizations and the Authority to encourage and facilitate the transfer to developing States, their nationals and the Enterprise of skills and marine technology with regard to activities in the Area.

ARTICLE 274

Objectives of the Authority

Subject to all legitimate interests including, *inter alia*, the rights and duties of holders, suppliers and recipients of technology, the Authority, with regard to activities in the Area, shall ensure that:

(a) on the basis of the principle of equitable geographical distribution, nationals of developing States, whether coastal, landlocked or geographically disadvantaged, shall be taken on for the purposes of training as members of the managerial, research and technical staff constituted for its undertakings;

(b) the technical documentation on the relevant equipment, machinery, devices and processes is made available to all States, in particular developing States which may need and request technical assistance in this field;

(c) adequate provision is made by the Authority to facilitate the acquisition of technical assistance in the field of marine technology by States which may need and request it, in particular developing States, and the acquisition by their nationals of the necessary skills and know-how, including professional training;

(d) States which may need and request technical assistance in this field, in particular developing States, are assisted in the acquisition of necessary equipment, processes, plant and other technical know-how through any financial arrangements provided for in this Convention.

SECTION 3. NATIONAL AND REGIONAL MARINE SCIENTIFIC AND TECHNOLOGICAL CENTRES

ARTICLE 275

Establishment of national centres

1. States, directly or through competent international organizations and the Authority, shall promote the establishment, particularly in developing coastal States, of national marine scientific and technological research centres and the strengthening of existing national centres, in order to stimulate and advance the conduct of marine scientific research by developing coastal States and to enhance their national capabilities to utilize and preserve their marine resources for their economic benefit.
2. States, through competent international organizations and the Authority, shall give adequate support to facilitate the establishment and strengthening of such national centres so as to provide for advanced training facilities and necessary equipment, skills and know-how as well as technical experts to such States which may need and request such assistance.

ARTICLE 276

Establishment of regional centres

1. States, in coordination with the competent international organizations, the Authority and national marine scientific and technological research institutions, shall promote the establishment of regional marine scientific and technological research centres, particularly in developing States, in order to stimulate and advance the conduct of marine scientific research by developing States and foster the transfer of marine technology.
2. All States of a region shall cooperate with the regional centres therein to ensure the more effective achievement of their objectives.

ARTICLE 277

Functions of regional centres

The functions of such regional centres shall include, *inter alia*:

(a) training and educational programmes at all levels on various aspects of marine scientific and technological research, particularly marine biology, including conservation and management of living resources, oceanography, hydrography, engineering, geological exploration of the seabed, mining and desalination technologies;

(b) management studies;

(c) study programmes related to the protection and preservation of the marine environment and the prevention, reduction and control of pollution;

(d) organization of regional conferences, seminars and symposia;

(e) acquisition and processing of marine scientific and technological data and information;

(f) prompt dissemination of results of marine scientific and technological research in readily available publications;

(g) publicizing national policies with regard to the transfer of marine technology and systematic comparative study of those policies;

(h) compilation and systematization of information on the marketing of technology and on contracts and other arrangements concerning patents; and

(i) technical cooperation with other States of the region.

SECTION 4. COOPERATION AMONG INTERNATIONAL ORGANIZATIONS

ARTICLE 278

Cooperation among international organizations

The competent international organizations, referred to in this Part and in Part XIII, shall take all appropriate measures to ensure, either directly or in close cooperation among themselves, the effective discharge of their functions and responsibilities under this Part.

LAW OF SEA CONVENTION, 1982

PART-XV

Settlement of Disputes

SECTION 1. GENERAL PROVISIONS

ARTICLE 279

Obligation to settle disputes by peaceful means

States Parties shall settle any dispute between them concerning the interpretation or application of this Convention by peaceful means in accordance with Article 2, paragraph 3, of the Charter of the United Nations and, to this end, shall seek a solution by the means indicated in Article 33, paragraph 1, of the Charter.

ARTICLE 280

Settlement of disputes by any peaceful means chosen by the parties

Nothing in this Part impairs the right of any States Parties to agree at any time to settle a dispute between them concerning the interpretation or application of this Convention by any peaceful means of their own choice.

ARTICLE 281

Procedure where no settlement has been reached by the parties

1. If the States Parties which are parties to a dispute concerning the interpretation or application of this Convention have agreed to seek settlement of the dispute by a peaceful means of their own choice, the procedures provided for in this Part apply only where no settlement has been reached by recourse to such means and the agreement between the parties does not exclude any further procedure.
2. If the parties have also agreed on a time-limit, paragraph 1 applies only upon the expiration of that time-limit.

ARTICLE 282

Obligations under general, regional or bilateral agreements

If the States Parties which are parties to a dispute concerning the interpretation or application of this Convention have agreed, through a general, regional or bilateral agreement or otherwise, that such dispute shall, at the request of any party to the dispute, be submitted to a procedure that entails a binding decision, that procedure shall apply in lieu of the procedures provided for in this Part, unless the parties to the dispute otherwise agree.

ARTICLE 283

Obligation to exchange views

1. When a dispute arises between States Parties concerning the interpretation or application of this Convention, the parties to the dispute shall proceed expeditiously to an exchange of views regarding its settlement by negotiation or other peaceful means.
2. The parties shall also proceed expeditiously to an exchange of views where a procedure for the settlement of such a dispute has been terminated without a settlement or where a settlement has been reached and the circumstances require consultation regarding the manner of implementing the settlement.

ARTICLE 284

Conciliation

1. A State Party which is a party to a dispute concerning the interpretation or application of this Convention may invite the other party or parties to submit the dispute to conciliation in accordance with the procedure under Annex V, section 1, or another conciliation procedure.
2. If the invitation is accepted and if the parties agree upon the conciliation procedure to be applied, any party may submit the dispute to that procedure.
3. If the invitation is not accepted or the parties do not agree upon the procedure, the conciliation proceedings shall be deemed to be terminated.

4. Unless the parties otherwise agree, when a dispute has been submitted to conciliation, the proceedings may be terminated only in accordance with the agreed conciliation procedure.

ARTICLE 285

Application of this section to disputes submitted pursuant to Part XI

This section applies to any dispute which pursuant to Part XI, section 5, is to be settled in accordance with procedures provided for in this Part. If an entity other than a State Party is a party to such a dispute, this section applies *mutatis mutandis.*

SECTION 2. COMPULSORY PROCEDURES ENTAILING BINDING DECISIONS

ARTICLE 286

Application of procedures under this section

Subject to section 3, any dispute concerning the interpretation or application of this Convention shall, where no settlement has been reached by recourse to section 1, be submitted at the request of any party to the dispute to the court or tribunal having jurisdiction under this section.

ARTICLE 287

Choice of procedure

1. When signing, ratifying or acceding to this Convention or at any time thereafter, a State shall be free to choose, by means of a written declaration, one or more of the following means for the settlement of disputes concerning the interpretation or application of this Convention:
   (a) the International Tribunal for the Law of the Sea established in accordance with Annex VI;
   (b) the International Court of Justice;
   (c) an arbitral tribunal constituted in accordance with Annex VII;
   (d) a special arbitral tribunal constituted in accordance with Annex VIII for one or more of the categories of disputes specified therein.

2. A declaration, made under paragraph 1, shall not affect or be affected by the obligation of a State Party to accept the jurisdiction of the Seabed Disputes Chamber of the International Tribunal for the Law of the Sea to the extent and in the manner provided for in Part XI, section 5.
3. A State Party, which is a party to a dispute not covered by a declaration in force, shall be deemed to have accepted arbitration in accordance with Annex VII.
4. If the parties to a dispute have accepted the same procedure for the settlement of the dispute, it may be submitted only to that procedure, unless the parties otherwise agree.
5. If the parties to a dispute have not accepted the same procedure for the settlement of the dispute, it may be submitted only to arbitration in accordance with Annex VII, unless the parties otherwise agree.
6. A declaration made under paragraph 1, shall remain in force until three months after notice of revocation has been deposited with the Secretary-General of the United Nations.
7. A new declaration, a notice of revocation or the expiry of a declaration does not in anyway affect proceedings pending before a court or tribunal having jurisdiction under this article, unless the parties otherwise agree.
8. Declarations and notices referred to in this article shall be deposited with the Secretary-General of the United Nations, who shall transmit copies thereof to the States Parties.

ARTICLE 288

Jurisdiction

1. A court or tribunal referred to in article 287 shall have jurisdiction over any dispute concerning the interpretation or application of this Convention which is submitted to it in accordance with this Part.
2. A court or tribunal referred to in article 287 shall also have jurisdiction over any dispute concerning the interpretation or application of an international

agreement related to the purposes of this Convention, which is submitted to it in accordance with the agreement.

3. The Seabed Disputes Chamber of the International Tribunal for the Law of the Sea established in accordance with Annex VI, and any other chamber or arbitral tribunal referred to in Part XI, section 5, shall have jurisdiction in any matter which is submitted to it in accordance therewith.
4. In the event of a dispute as to whether a court or tribunal has jurisdiction, the matter shall be settled by decision of that court or tribunal.

ARTICLE 289

Experts

In any dispute involving scientific or technical matters, a court or tribunal exercising jurisdiction under this section may, at the request of a party or *proprio motu*, select in consultation with the parties no fewer than two scientific or technical experts chosen preferably from the relevant list prepared in accordance with Annex VIII, article 2, to sit with the court or tribunal but without the right to vote.

ARTICLE 290

Provisional measures

1. If a dispute has been duly submitted to a court or tribunal which considers that *prima facie* it has jurisdiction under this Part or Part XI, section 5, the court or tribunal may prescribe any provisional measures, which it considers appropriate, under the circumstances to preserve the respective rights of the parties to the dispute or to prevent serious harm to the marine environment, pending the final decision.
2. Provisional measures may be modified or revoked as soon as the circumstances justifying them have changed or ceased to exist.
3. Provisional measures may be prescribed, modified or revoked, under this article, only at the request of a party to the dispute and after the parties have been given an opportunity to be heard.

4. The court or tribunal shall forthwith give notice to the parties to the dispute, and to such other States Parties as it considers appropriate, of the prescription, modification or revocation of provisional measures.
5. Pending the constitution of an arbitral tribunal to which a dispute is being submitted under this section, any court or tribunal agreed upon by the parties or, failing such agreement within two weeks from the date of the request for provisional measures, the International Tribunal for the Law of the Sea or, with respect to activities in the Area, the Seabed Disputes Chamber, may prescribe, modify or revoke provisional measures, in accordance with this article, if it considers that *prima facie* the tribunal which is to be constituted would have jurisdiction and that the urgency of the situation so requires. Once constituted, the tribunal to which the dispute has been submitted may modify, revoke or affirm those provisional measures, acting in conformity with paragraphs 1 to 4.
6. The parties to the dispute shall comply promptly with any provisional measures prescribed under this article.

ARTICLE 291

Access

1. All the dispute settlement procedures specified in this Part shall be open to States Parties.
2. The dispute settlement procedures specified in this Part shall be open to entities other than States Parties only as specifically provided for in this Convention.

ARTICLE 292

Prompt release of vessels and crews

1. Where the authorities of a State Party have detained a vessel flying the flag of another State Party and it is alleged that the detaining State has not complied with the provisions of this Convention for the prompt release of the vessel or its crew upon the posting of a reasonable bond or other financial security, the question of release from detention may be submitted to any court or

tribunal agreed upon by the parties or, failing such agreement within 10 days from the time of detention, to a court or tribunal accepted by the detaining State under article 287 or to the International Tribunal for the Law of the Sea, unless the parties otherwise agree.

2. The application for release may be made only by or on behalf of the flag State of the vessel.
3. The court or tribunal shall deal without delay with the application for release and shall deal only with the question of release, without prejudice to the merits of any case before the appropriate domestic forum against the vessel, its owner or its crew. The authorities of the detaining State remain competent to release the vessel or its crew at any time.
4. Upon the posting of the bond or other financial security determined by the court or tribunal, the authorities of the detaining State shall comply promptly with the decision of the court or tribunal concerning the release of the vessel or its crew.

ARTICLE 293

Applicable law

1. A court or tribunal having jurisdiction under this section shall apply this Convention and other rules of international law not incompatible with this Convention.
2. Paragraph 1 does not prejudice the power of the court or tribunal having jurisdiction under this section to decide a case *ex aequo et bono*, if the parties so agree.

ARTICLE 294

Preliminary proceedings

1. A court or tribunal provided for in article 287 to which an application is made in respect of a dispute referred to in article 297 shall determine at the request of a party, or may determine *proprio motu*, whether the claim constitutes an abuse of legal process or whether *prima facie* it is well founded. If the court or tribunal determines that the claim constitutes an abuse of legal process or is *prima facie* unfounded, it shall take no further action in the case.

2. Upon receipt of the application, the court or tribunal shall immediately notify the other party or parties of the application, and shall fix a reasonable time-limit within which they may request it to make a determination in accordance with paragraph 1.
3. Nothing in this article affects the right of any party to a dispute to make preliminary objections in accordance with the applicable rules of procedure.

ARTICLE 295

Exhaustion of local remedies

Any dispute between States Parties concerning the interpretation or application of this Convention may be submitted to the procedures provided for in this section only after local remedies have been exhausted where this is required by international law.

ARTICLE 296

Finality and binding force of decisions

1. Any decision rendered by a court or tribunal having jurisdiction under this section shall be final and shall be complied with by all the parties to the dispute.
2. Any such decision shall have no binding force except between the parties and in respect of that particular dispute.

SECTION 3. LIMITATIONS AND EXCEPTIONS TO APPLICABILITY OF SECTION 2

ARTICLE 297

Limitations on applicability of section 2

1. Disputes concerning the interpretation or application of this Convention with regard to the exercise by a coastal State of its sovereign rights or jurisdiction provided for in this Convention shall be subject to the procedures provided for in section 2 in the following cases:
   (a) when it is alleged that a coastal State has acted in contravention of the provisions of this Convention in regard to the freedoms and rights of navigation,

overflight or the laying of submarine cables and pipelines, or in regard to other internationally lawful uses of the sea specified in article 58;

(b) when it is alleged that a State in exercising the aforementioned freedoms, rights or uses has acted in contravention of this Convention or of laws or regulations adopted by the coastal State in conformity with this Convention and other rules of international law not incompatible with this Convention; or

(c) when it is alleged that a coastal State has acted in contravention of specified international rules and standards for the protection and preservation of the marine environment which are applicable to the coastal State and which have been established by this Convention or through a competent international organization or diplomatic conference in accordance with this Convention.

2. (a) Disputes concerning the interpretation or application of the provisions of this Convention with regard to marine scientific research shall be settled in accordance with section 2, except that the coastal State shall not be obliged to accept the submission to such settlement of any dispute arising out of —

(i) the exercise by the coastal State of a right or discretion in accordance with article 246; or

(ii) a decision by the coastal State to order suspension or cessation of a research project in accordance with article 253.

(b) A dispute arising from an allegation by the researching State that with respect to a specific project the coastal State is not exercising its rights under articles 246 and 253 in a manner compatible with this Convention shall be submitted, at the request of either party, to conciliation under Annex V, section 2, provided that the conciliation commission shall not call in question the exercise by the coastal State of its discretion to designate specific areas as referred to in article 246, paragraph 6, or of its discretion to withhold consent in accordance with article 246, paragraph 5.

3. (a) Disputes concerning the interpretation or application of the provisions of this Convention with regard to fisheries shall be settled in accordance with section 2, except that the coastal State shall not be obliged to accept the submission to such settlement of any dispute relating to its sovereign rights with respect to the living resources in the exclusive economic zone or their exercise, including its discretionary powers for determining the allowable catch, its harvesting capacity, the allocation of surpluses to other States and the terms and conditions established in its conservation and management laws and regulations.

(b) Where no settlement has been reached by recourse to section 1 of this Part, a dispute shall be submitted to conciliation under Annex V, section 2, at the request of any party to the dispute, when it is alleged that:

(i) a coastal State has manifestly failed to comply with its obligations to ensure through proper conservation and management measures that the maintenance of the living resources in the exclusive economic zone is not seriously endangered;

(ii) a coastal State has arbitrarily refused to determine, at the request of another State, the allowable catch and its capacity to harvest living resources with respect to stocks which that other State is interested in fishing; or

(iii) a coastal State has arbitrarily refused to allocate to any State, under articles 62, 69 and 70 and under the terms and conditions established by the coastal State consistent with this Convention, the whole or part of the surplus it has declared to exist.

(c) In no case shall the conciliation commission substitute its discretion for that of the coastal State.

(d) The report of the conciliation commission shall be communicated to the appropriate international organizations.

(e) In negotiating agreements pursuant to articles 69 and 70, States Parties, unless they otherwise agree, shall include a clause on measures which they shall take in order to minimize the possibility of a disagreement concerning the interpretation or application of the agreement, and on how they should proceed if a disagreement nevertheless arises.

ARTICLE 298

Optional exceptions to applicability of section 2

1. When signing, ratifying or acceding to this Convention or at any time thereafter, a State may, without prejudice to the obligations arising under section 1, declare in writing that it does not accept any one or more of the procedures provided for in section 2 with respect to one or more of the following categories of disputes:

(a) (i) disputes concerning the interpretation or application of articles 15, 74 and 83 relating to sea boundary delimitations, or those involving historic bays or titles, provided that a State having made such a declaration shall, when such a dispute arises subsequent to the entry into force of this Convention and where no agreement within a reasonable period of time is reached in negotiations between the parties, at the request of any party to the dispute, accept submission of the matter to conciliation under Annex V, section 2; and provided further that any dispute that necessarily involves the concurrent consideration of any unsettled dispute concerning sovereignty or other rights over continental or insular land territory shall be excluded from such submission,

(ii) after the conciliation commission has presented its report, which shall state the reasons on which it is based, the parties shall negotiate an agreement on the basis of that report; if these negotiations do not result in an agreement, the parties shall, by mutual consent, submit the question to one of the procedures provided for in section 2, unless the parties otherwise agree,

(iii) this subparagraph does not apply to any sea boundary dispute finally settled by an arrangement between the parties, or to any such dispute which is to be settled in accordance with a bilateral or multilateral agreement binding upon those parties;

(b) disputes concerning military activities, including military activities by government vessels and aircraft engaged in non-commercial service, and disputes concerning law enforcement activities in regard to the exercise of sovereign rights or jurisdiction excluded from the jurisdiction of a court or tribunal under article 297, paragraph 2 or 3; or

(c) disputes in respect of which the Security Council of the United Nations is exercising the functions assigned to it by the Charter of the United Nations, unless the Security Council decides to remove the matter from its agenda or calls upon the parties to settle it by the means provided for in this Convention.

2. A State Party which has made a declaration under paragraph 1 may, at any time, withdraw it, or agree to submit a dispute excluded by such declaration to any procedure specified in this Convention.

3. A State Party which has made a declaration under paragraph 1 shall not be entitled to submit any dispute falling within the excepted category of disputes to any

procedure in this Convention as against another State Party, without the consent of that party.

4. If one of the States Parties has made a declaration under paragraph 1(a), any other State Party may submit any dispute falling within an excepted category against the declarant party to the procedure specified in such declaration.
5. A new declaration, or the withdrawal of a declaration, does not in anyway affect proceedings pending before a court or tribunal in accordance with this article, unless the parties otherwise agree.
6. Declarations and notices of withdrawal of declarations, under this article, shall be deposited with the Secretary-General of the United Nations, who shall transmit copies thereof to the States Parties.

ARTICLE 299

Right of the parties to agree upon a procedure

1. A dispute excluded under article 297 or excepted by a declaration made under article 298 from the dispute settlement procedures provided for in section 2 may be submitted to such procedures only by agreement of the parties to the dispute.
2. Nothing in this section impairs the right of the parties to the dispute to agree to some other procedure for the settlement of such dispute or to reach an amicable settlement.

LAW OF SEA CONVENTION, 1982

PART-XVI

General Provisions

ARTICLE 300

Good faith and abuse of rights

States Parties shall fulfil in good faith the obligations assumed under this Convention and shall exercise the rights, jurisdiction and freedoms recognized in this Convention in a manner which would not constitute an abuse of right.

ARTICLE 301

Peaceful uses of the seas

In exercising their rights and performing their duties under this Convention, States Parties shall refrain from any threat or use of force against the territorial integrity or political independence of any State, or in any other manner inconsistent with the principles of international law embodied in the Charter of the United Nations.

ARTICLE 302

Disclosure of information

Without prejudice to the right of a State Party to resort to the procedures for the settlement of disputes provided for in this Convention, nothing in this Convention shall be deemed to require a State Party, in the fulfilment of its obligations under this Convention, to supply information the disclosure of which is contrary to the essential interests of its security.

ARTICLE 303

Archaeological and historical objects found at sea

1. States have the duty to protect objects of an archaeological and historical nature found at sea, and shall cooperate for this purpose.
2. In order to control traffic in such objects, the coastal State may, in applying article 33, presume that their

removal from the seabed in the zone referred to in that article without its approval would result in an infringement within its territory or territorial sea of the laws and regulations referred to in that article.

3. Nothing in this article affects the rights of identifiable owners, the law of salvage or other rules of admiralty, or laws and practices with respect to cultural exchanges.
4. This article is without prejudice to other international agreements and rules of international law regarding the protection of objects of an archaeological and historical nature.

ARTICLE 304

Responsibility and liability for damage

The provisions of this Convention regarding responsibility and liability for damage are without prejudice to the application of existing rules and the development of further rules regarding responsibility and liability under international law.

LAW OF SEA CONVENTION, 1982

PART-XVII

Final Provisions

ARTICLE 305

Signature

1. This Convention shall be open for signature by:
   (a) all States;
   (b) Namibia, represented by the United Nations Council for Namibia;
   (c) all self-governing associated States which have chosen that status in an act of self-determination supervised and approved by the United Nations in accordance with General Assembly resolution 1514 (XV) and which have competence over the matters governed by this Convention, including the competence to enter into treaties in respect of those matters;
   (d) all self-governing associated States which, in accordance with their respective instruments of association, have competence over the matters governed by this Convention, including the competence to enter into treaties in respect of those matters;
   (e) all territories which enjoy full internal self-government, recognized as such by the United Nations, but have not attained full independence in accordance with General Assembly resolution 1514 (XV) and which have competence over the matters governed by this Convention, including the competence to enter into treaties in respect of those matters; and
   (f) international organizations, in accordance with Annex IX.
2. This Convention shall remain open for signature until

9th December 1984, at the Ministry of Foreign Affairs of Jamaica and also, from 1st July 1983 until 9th December 1984, at United Nations Headquarters in New York.

ARTICLE 306

Ratification and formal confirmation

This Convention is subject to ratification by States and the other entities referred to in article 305, paragraph l(b), (c), (d) and (e), and to formal confirmation, in accordance with Annex IX, by the entities referred to in article 305, paragraph 1. The instruments of ratification and of formal confirmation shall be deposited with the Secretary-General of the United Nations.

ARTICLE 307

Accession

This Convention shall remain open for accession by States and the other entities referred to in article 305. Accession by the entities referred to in article 305, paragraph 1, shall be in accordance with Annex IX. The instruments of accession shall be deposited with the Secretary-General of the United Nations.

ARTICLE 308

Entry into force

1. This Convention shall enter into force 12 months after the date of deposit of the sixtieth instrument of ratification or accession.
2. For each State ratifying or acceding to this Convention after the deposit of the sixtieth instrument of ratification or accession, the Convention shall enter into force on the thirtieth day following the deposit of its instrument of ratification or accession, subject to paragraph 1.
3. The Assembly of the Authority shall meet on the date of entry into force of this Convention and shall elect the Council of the Authority. The first Council shall be constituted in a manner consistent with the purpose of article 161 if the provisions of that article cannot be strictly applied.
4. The rules, regulations and procedures drafted by the Preparatory Commission shall apply provisionally

pending their formal adoption by the Authority, in accordance with Part XI.

5. The Authority and its organs shall act in accordance with resolution II of the Third United Nations Conference on the Law of the Sea relating to preparatory investment and with decisions of the Preparatory Commission taken pursuant to that resolution.

ARTICLE 309

Reservations and exceptions

No reservations or exceptions may be made to this Convention unless expressly permitted by other articles of this Convention.

ARTICLE 310

Declarations and statements

Article 309 does not preclude a State, when signing, ratifying or acceding to this Convention, from making declarations or statements, however phrased or named, with a view, *inter alia,* to the harmonization of its laws and regulations with the provisions of this Convention, provided that such declarations or statements do not purport to exclude or to modify the legal effect of the provisions of this Convention in their application to that State.

ARTICLE 311

Relation to other conventions and international agreements

1. This Convention shall prevail, as between States Parties, over the Geneva Conventions on the Law of the Sea of 29th April 1958.
2. This Convention shall not alter the rights and obligations of States Parties which arise from other agreements compatible with this Convention and which do not affect the enjoyment by other States Parties of their rights or the performance of their obligations under this Convention.
3. Two or more States Parties may conclude agreements modifying or suspending the operation of provisions of this Convention, applicable solely to the relations

between them, provided that such agreements do not relate to a provision derogation from which is incompatible with the effective execution of the object and purpose of this Convention, and provided further that such agreements shall not affect the application of the basic principles embodied herein, and that the provisions of such agreements do not affect the enjoyment by other States Parties of their rights or the performance of their obligations under this Convention.

4. States Parties intending to conclude an agreement, referred to in paragraph 3, shall notify the other States Parties through the depositary of this Convention of their intention to conclude the agreement and of the modification or suspension for which it provides.
5. This article does not affect international agreements expressly permitted or preserved by other articles of this Convention.
6. States Parties agree that there shall be no amendments to the basic principle relating to the common heritage of mankind set forth in article 136 and that they shall not be party to any agreement in derogation thereof.

ARTICLE 312

Amendment

1. After the expiry of a period of 10 years from the date of entry into force of this Convention, a State Party may, by written communication addressed to the Secretary-General of the United Nations, propose specific amendments to this Convention, other than those relating to activities in the Area, and request the convening of a conference to consider such proposed amendments. The Secretary-General shall circulate such communication to all States Parties. If, within 12 months from the date of the circulation of the communication, not less than one half of the States Parties reply favourably to the request, the Secretary-General shall convene the conference.
2. The decision-making procedure applicable at the amendment conference shall be the same as that

applicable at the Third United Nations Conference on the Law of the Sea unless otherwise decided by the conference. The conference should make every effort to reach agreement on any amendments by way of consensus and there should be no voting on them until all efforts at consensus have been exhausted.

ARTICLE 313

Amendment by simplified procedure

1. A State Party may, by written communication addressed to the Secretary-General of the United Nations, propose an amendment to this Convention, other than an amendment relating to activities in the Area, to be adopted by the simplified procedure set forth in this article without convening a conference. The Secretary-General shall circulate the communication to all States Parties.
2. If, within a period of 12 months from the date of the circulation of the communication, a State Party objects to the proposed amendment or to the proposal for its adoption by the simplified procedure, the amendment shall be considered rejected. The Secretary-General shall immediately notify all States Parties accordingly.
3. If, 12 months from the date of the circulation of the communication, no State Party has objected to the proposed amendment or to the proposal for its adoption by the simplified procedure, the proposed amendment shall be considered adopted. The Secretary-General shall notify all States Parties that the proposed amendment has been adopted.

ARTICLE 314

Amendments to the provisions of this Convention relating exclusively to activities in the Area

1. A State Party may, by written communication addressed to the Secretary-General of the Authority, propose an amendment to the provisions of this Convention relating exclusively to activities in the Area, including Annex VI, section 4. The Secretary-General shall circulate such communication to all States Parties. The proposed

amendment shall be subject to approval by the Assembly, following its approval by the Council. Representatives of States Parties in those organs shall have full powers to consider and approve the proposed amendment. The proposed amendment as approved by the Council and the Assembly shall be considered adopted.

2. Before approving any amendment under paragraph 1, the Council and the Assembly shall ensure that it does not prejudice the system of exploration for and exploitation of the resources of the Area, pending the Review Conference in accordance with article 155.

ARTICLE 315

Signature, ratification of, accession to and authentic texts of amendments

1. Once adopted, amendments to this Convention shall be open for signature by States Parties for 12 months from the date of adoption, at United Nations Headquarters in New York, unless otherwise provided in the amendment itself.
2. Articles 306, 307 and 320 apply to all amendments to this Convention.

ARTICLE 316

Entry into force of amendments

1. Amendments to this Convention, other than those referred to in paragraph 5, shall enter into force for the States Parties ratifying or acceding to them on the thirtieth day following the deposit of instruments of ratification or accession by two thirds of the States Parties or by 60 States Parties, whichever is greater. Such amendments shall not affect the enjoyment by other States Parties of their rights or the performance of their obligations under this Convention.
2. An amendment may provide that a larger number of ratifications or accessions shall be required for its entry into force than are required by this article.
3. For each State Party ratifying or acceding to an amendment, referred to in paragraph 1, after the deposit of the required number of instruments of ratification

or accession, the amendment shall enter into force on the thirtieth day following the deposit of its instrument of ratification or accession.

4. A State which becomes a Party to this Convention after the entry into force of an amendment, in accordance with paragraph 1, shall, failing an expression of a different intention by that State:
   (a) be considered as a Party to this Convention as so amended; and
   (b) be considered as a Party to the unamended Convention in relation to any State Party not bound by the amendment.
5. Any amendment relating exclusively to activities in the Area and any amendment to Annex VI shall enter into force for all States Parties one year following the deposit of instruments of ratification or accession by three-fourths of the States Parties.
6. A State which becomes a Party to this Convention after the entry into force of amendments, in accordance with paragraph 5, shall be considered as a Party to this Convention as so amended.

ARTICLE 317

Denunciation

1. A State Party may, by written notification addressed to the Secretary-General of the United Nations, denounce this Convention and may indicate its reasons. Failure to indicate reasons shall not affect the validity of the denunciation. The denunciation shall take effect one year after the date of receipt of the notification, unless the notification specifies a later date.
2. A State shall not be discharged by reason of the denunciation from the financial and contractual obligations which accrued while it was a Party to this Convention, nor shall the denunciation affect any right, obligation or legal situation of that State created through the execution of this Convention prior to its termination for that State.

3. The denunciation shall not in anyway affect the duty of any State Party to fulfil any obligation embodied in this Convention to which it would be subject under international law independently of this Convention.

ARTICLE 318

Status of Annexes

The Annexes form an integral part of this Convention and, unless expressly provided otherwise, a reference to this Convention or to one of its Parts includes a reference to the Annexes relating thereto.

ARTICLE 319

Depositary

1. The Secretary-General of the United Nations shall be the depositary of this Convention and amendments thereto.
2. In addition to his functions as depositary, the Secretary-General shall:
   (a) report to all States Parties, the Authority and the competent international organizations on issues of a general nature that have arisen with respect to this Convention;
   (b) notify the Authority of ratifications and formal confirmations of and accessions to this Convention and amendments thereto, as well as of denunciations of this Convention;
   (c) notify States Parties of agreements in accordance with article 311, paragraph 4;
   (d) circulate amendments adopted, in accordance with this Convention, to States Parties for ratification or accession; and
   (e) convene necessary meetings of the States Parties in accordance with this Convention.
3. (a) The Secretary-General shall also transmit to the observers referred to in article 156:
      (i) reports referred to in paragraph 2(a);
      (ii) notifications referred to in paragraph 2(b) and (c); and

(iii) texts of amendments referred to in paragraph 2(d), for their information.

(b) The Secretary-General shall also invite those observers to participate as observers at meetings of States Parties referred to in paragraph 2(e).

ARTICLE 320

Authentic texts

The original of this Convention, of which the Arabic, Chinese, English, French, Russian and Spanish texts are equally authentic, shall, subject to article 305, paragraph 2, be deposited with the Secretary-General of the United Nations.

IN WITNESS WHEREOF, the undersigned Plenipotentiaries, being duly authorized thereto, have signed this Convention.

DONE AT MONTEGO BAY, this tenth day of December, one thousand nine hundred and eighty-two.